D1638483

A Penguin Special
Operation Thunder: the Entebbe Raid

Yehuda Ofer was the Deputy Editor of the Israel Air Force magazine for twenty years and specializes in writing about military affairs. In the course of writing *Operation Thunder* he was able to interview the main participants, and to have access to sources that were not released to other journalists. Yehuda Ofer has published several books on army and aviation subjects in Israel, and is the aviation correspondent of a number of newspapers in Israel and overseas.

Yehuda Ofer Operation Thunder:
the Entebbe Raid

The Israelis' Own Story
Translated by Julian Meltzer

Penguin Books

Penguin Books Ltd,
Harmondsworth, Middlesex, England
Penguin Books,
625 Madison Avenue, New York, New York 10022, U.S.A.
Penguin Books Australia Ltd,
Ringwood, Victoria, Australia
Penguin Books Canada Ltd,
41 Steelcase Road West, Markham, Ontario, Canada
Penguin Books (N.Z.) Ltd,
182–190 Wairau Road, Auckland 10, New Zealand

First published in Hebrew as *Operation Jonathan: Liberation from Entebbe*
by Massada Press, Tel Aviv 1976
Published in Penguin Books 1976

Made and printed in Great Britain by
Cox & Wyman Ltd, London, Reading and Fakenham
Set in Intertype Times

Contents

List of Illustrations

Acknowledgements

The author desires to express his deep and sincere gratitude to Mr Alexander Peli, President of Massada Press, who by his welcome initiative provided the incentive to write this book. Particular thanks are due to Ms Minna Eiger, whose many talents were of great assistance.

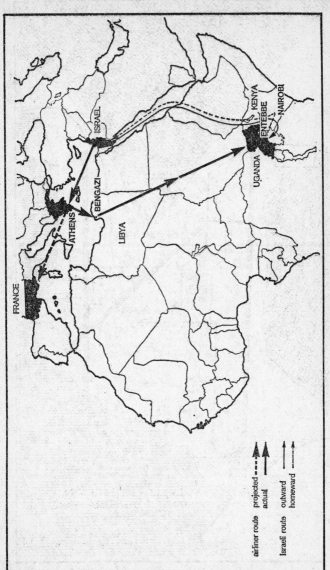

1 The route of the Air France airliner

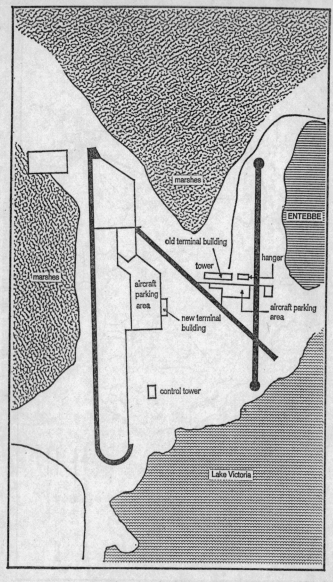

2   The operations area at Entebbe

1 The Snatch

Exactly at noon on Sunday, 27 June 1976, the long silver shape of the airliner lifted off the burning runway of the international airport at Athens with 246 passengers in its broad belly, and soared off on its nonstop flight to Paris. It carried an aircrew of twelve.

One of the wide comfortable seats was occupied by Joseph Abougedir, a Tunis-born Israeli aged forty-eight, father of seven children. Two passengers who had boarded the plane at Athens sat beside him and, in doing so, muttered a greeting in a language he did not understand.

A few moments later one of his new companions proffered a box of dates, gesturing to him to take one. Abougedir glanced at the Arabic label and saw that the dates came from Iraq. He took one and began munching it. Apart from the box, the two strangers had other boxes and bulging handbags.

A few rows away from Abougedir in the broad passenger cabin of the French 'air-bus' plane sat Mrs Rina Cooper and her husband, Yerach. Both were holiday-bound for Europe. Rina thought about the party which a friend at work had thrown for her the night before. Some of the guests had joked, 'Watch out for terrorists'. She promised to be on the alert.

Dora Bloch, a seventy-five-year-old widow, resident of a prosperous middle class suburb of western Jerusalem, was another passenger on the same Air France plane – Flight 139 from Tel Aviv to Paris. She was *en route* to New York for the wedding of her son, Daniel Bloch, a well-known

Israeli newsman. Another son, her oldest, Ilan Har-Tuv, sat beside her.

A short while earlier, when the plane was still on the ground in Athens, Mrs Bloch had whispered to her son, 'Look at those two sitting at the back. I think they're Arabs'. Ilan slanted a glance at the pair who had aroused his mother's suspicions, and saw that they were carrying long cases of the kind used to hold automatic weapons.

Another passenger who had ill-forebodings was Sarah Davidson, travelling with her husband, Arieh, and their two sons, Ron and Bennie. The family were on their way to the United States for a coast-to-coast tour.

When her husband bought the air tickets in Tel Aviv, he did not know that the plane would make an interim landing in Athens. He learned of it only when the family were in the waiting hall at Ben-Gurion Airport. When he had told her of it at the airport early that morning, she replied at once, insistently, 'Let's not go on the plane. We don't know who's likely to get on in Athens'. She tried to persuade him to put off the trip and switch to an El Al aircraft, but eventually gave in so as not to spoil their long-anticipated trip.

Rina's suspicions were renewed with even greater intensity while they were still on the ground at Athens airport. She saw that the door to the pilot's cabin was wide open, and anyone who wanted to do so entered freely. The passengers had boarded without any prior body-check. She recognized clearly a number of Arabs among those who joined the plane. Her bad premonitions came back now that the aircraft was flying in the clear skies over the blue waters of the Mediterranean, strewn with a pendant of white islands sparkling in the sunshine far below.

About ninety minutes after the French air-bus had taken off from Athens, the door of the conference room in the Israeli Prime Minister's offices in Jerusalem opened and the Mili-

2

tary Secretary to the Prime Minister, Brigadier-General Poren, came in purposefully and passed a note to Itzhak Rabin.

This was no extraordinary occurrence and the other ministers grouped around the long table paid no attention to the interruption. But suddenly they were gripped by a change in the Prime Minister's expression as his eyes skimmed over the piece of paper. He halted the meeting and told his colleagues of the contents: the Air France aircraft which had left Ben-Gurion Aiport that morning had been hijacked after taking off from Athens. A wireless message, received a few minutes earlier from the flight controller at the international airport tower in Israel, said simply:

Air France Flight 139 which left Israel this morning and landed at Athens *en route* to Paris disappeared after take-off at 12.30. All contact lost with it and all that is known is that the plane turned southeastwards.

Who was behind the hijacking? Who had ordered the captain of the aircraft to change course? These questions hovered in the hall as the Cabinet meeting continued amid an air of tense expectancy waiting for further information.

Eight minutes after the plane took off from Athens, Joseph Haddad, a resident of Bat-Yam, a seaside resort south of Tel Aviv, married and the father of three small children, sat deep in thought. This was no holiday trip for him. He had been planning to emigrate from Israel.

Haddad could not take it any more: his job was difficult, he had to answer frequent call-ups for reserve army service, new and burdensome taxes kept cropping up from time-to-time. He had come from Tunisia to Israel some twenty-two years earlier and had earned his living as a bread roundsman. After much heart searching, he had decided to utilize the occasion of his wedding to his wife's cousin, Lizette, to

3

probe the possibilities of finding employment abroad. Lizette was young – twenty-six years of age; he, too, was still young. They could build a new life. He would make a little money and return.

Still pensive, he caught a flutter out of the corner of his eye as a tall figure rose out of one of the seats and began yelling. Joseph was certain that the man had suddenly gone out of his mind.

At the same moment two other men started running down the aisle. One of them, a young man with long hair, was clad in a red shirt, grey trousers and a beige jacket. The other, with a massive moustache, adorning his countenance, wore long trousers and a yellow shirt. They ran at top speed towards the first-class cabin.

Within seconds, the air hostess burst out of the first-class section and, in spite of the alarm and shock, tried to calm the passengers with trembling gestures.

Two terrorists stood at the entrance of the first-class partition holding hand-grenades with the safety-catches up in one hand and revolvers in the other.

During the panic and uproar that ensued in those few seconds Joseph sneaked out of his seat, the one thought uppermost – *something has to be done*. Lizette, at his side, pulled his sleeve and pleaded with him to sit down. Her pleas were unavailing. Joseph was determined to jump them.

'What are you going to fight with?' Lizette cried. 'Your bare hands? They'll blow up the plane because of you.'

When she saw there was nothing to be done, she snatched up a carafe of water from the small ledge at her side and dashed the contents in her husband's face. He sat down.

A short, middle-aged man also tried to resist the hijackers. Their reprisal was swift and brutal: they threw him to the floor of the plane and beat him mercilessly. The young German woman hijacker outdid the others.

Bennie, thirteen-year-old son of Sarah Davidson, clung to his mother – '*Ima*, Mummy, I don't want to die yet, so soon'. Sarah placed a reassuring hand on his shoulder. 'We shan't die, Bennie, we'll get home, we'll return to Israel. We'll be together all the time.'

Ruth Gross, a lovely blonde, pushed her six-year-old son, Shai, under the seat, between her knees, and covered him with her skirt. She was afraid the hijackers would take him from her.

The captain of the aircraft, fifty-two-year-old Michel Bacos, a handsome Frenchman, married and with two children, sat on the left-hand side in the pilot's cabin near the controls.

The hardest part of the take-off was already behind him and he prepared for an easy, pleasant flight to Paris along air-routes with which he was familiar. Everything was relaxed.

Suddenly he heard a confused noise and shouting from the passenger cabin. His first thought was that a fire had broken out. Before he could send a swift glance over the dozens of dials on the panels in front of him, to check if all was well, a tall, blond man burst into the pilot's cabin. The blue-eyed, fair-skinned man held a pistol in his hand as he snapped in short, staccato sentences that the plane had been taken over and that the captain must change course for Libya.

Captain Bacos did as ordered and swung the aircraft in a wide arc southwards.

Rina Cooper, who had promised her friends to beware of terrorists, sat shrinking in her seat. Her first concern had been for her sister and brother-in-law who were sitting some distance away. She was afraid that the terrorists were going to murder the passengers one-by-one and would reach her sister and brother-in-law first.

At that moment the command came to raise hands. Without her knowing why, her hands refused to obey her and rise. It seemed humiliating to her. As a *sabra*, a native Israeli, she had never been tested in her life in a situation of this kind. Her heart contracted as she saw the other passengers putting up their hands in surrender.

She pushed her hands into her handbag and wriggled deeper into the seat. Her thoughts were sharply focused on her children, whom she had left at home in the care of her parents. Odd, but the one thought that stabbed into her mind like a red-hot sword was, 'If I die, then maybe my son will start taking his lessons seriously!'

Suddenly a voice came over the aircraft public address system. It spoke a fluent English with the trace of a German accent. 'This is Captain Basil Al-Kubeisi, of the Che Guevara Forces of the Commando of the Palestinian Liberation Forces. This plane has been hijacked. If you behave quietly, nothing bad will happen to you.'

From the accented voice of the hijacker, who pretended to be their new 'captain', the passengers knew that he was not an Arab.

During the long dragging days after the snatch of the airliner Sarah Davidson kept a record in her small pocket diary. She wrote in tiny letters:

'I cannot express my feelings in the first moments of a hijacked plane. It is impossible to find the words. We have been told to give up all handbags, all papers, all documents. They said they would conduct a personal body search of each one of us. It will not be pleasant for me ... I did not see a woman among the hijackers. I am terribly afraid of a body search, because of the special surgery I had. I have never hidden it from friends and acquaintances. I did not think it was a secret. But here ... with hijackers ...'

To Sarah's great relief, the hijackers for some reason stopped searching the persons of the passengers before they reached her.

The hijacking was carried out with systematic German precision. The 'captain' himself supervised every stage of the operation and relied on no one but himself. At first he ordered the passengers to change seats and the women and children to go into the first-class section forward, leaving the others in the 'tourist' class. Then he commanded all passengers to throw on the floor whatever firearms or weapons they had. Three pocket-knives and a number of forks were the sum total amassed.

Now came the turn of the documents. The German barked out that everyone should pass their documents to him without exception. Yet in spite of this the terrorist leader tried to reassure the travellers.

'Keep quiet for your own sakes. As long as nothing is done you won't be harmed. We don't want to kill any one of you. We are humanitarians.'

The travellers were destined to hear those last three words scores of times from him in the ensuing week.

While he was addressing them, two other hijackers were tying two boxes of explosives to the doors of the plane. One of them was a young Arab, and the second a be-spectacled girl with brown hair, whose face bore a demented expression.

The German hijackers' attempted reassurance failed to calm the passengers. An atmosphere of fear pervaded the cabin. Women screamed and children wept hysterically. Unable to reach the toilets some of the passengers relieved their needs where they sat, some in air-sickness bags, others on the floor.

During the flight the air-pirates allowed people to go to the toilets but compelled them to walk with their hands over their heads. There were cases where the German women entered the toilets after the males, jerked their coat-tails or shirts and urged them to hurry up and finish.

When the panic had subsided the terrorists made a brief announcement. 'From now on passengers must use the name "Arafat" instead of "Air France".'

There were four hijackers on the plane. As on previous occasions it seemed that the Arab terror organizations did not rely too much on their own compatriots but enlisted the help of foreigners. That was why the leader of the action was Wilfred Boese, a known anarchist with a long record of co-operation with the vicious arch-terrorist code-named 'Carlos'.

Boese had been detained by the French police the year before after the firing of a bazooka shell at a Yugoslav plane parked on the tarmac at Orly Airport in Paris. The plane was attacked in error, the real target having been an El Al aircraft.

Twenty-eight-year-old Boese with another German, Johannes Weinrich, hired the automobile used in the attack. But the French police authorities had insufficient evidence of his complicity and a short while later he was handed over to West Germany. He was detained but released soon after this and went underground.

Wilfred Boese was born on 1 January 1949 in West Germany and became a member of the Baader-Meinhof gang. He then switched to a terror group headed by the notorious Wadie Haddad. Boese was also known as Claudius Axel and belonged to a Socialist students' organization in West Germany.

He had also been arrested on 25 June 1973 in Paris by the French security police after having attempted to break into the apartment of a Lebanese named Michel Murkabel who, according to rumour, had betrayed his associates in a terrorist unit and become an informer in the pay of the French Sûreté.

Murkabel did not escape the fate decreed for him by his former comrades-in-arms; two days later, on 27 June 1975, he was shot dead by 'Carlos' when two French police inspectors came with him to the door of the arch-terrorist's apartment.

If this were not enough, it was also believed that Boese had a hand in the kidnapping of the O.P.E.C. oil-kingdoms' ministers who were attending a Sunday morning conference in Vienna.

In contrast to Boese, of whom full particulars were available, there are scant details about the identity of the woman hijacker, whom her captives described as 'a savage Nazi beast'. She insisted in the plane on being addressed by the name 'Halima'. During the hijacking she wore a blue skirt, light-blue shirtwaist, blue stockings and a wig, and she tried to be tougher than her male confederates.

'Halima' marched to and fro along the length of the aisles, and between the seats, one hand grasping a live grenade and the other scratching her head through the blonde wig she wore. There are a number of guesses concerning her real identity. The West German security services believed for a while that she was the widow of B. Hausmann, the German terrorist who was used by the terrorists as a 'live bomb'. Hausmann had been sent early in 1976 to Israel carrying a booby-trapped valise timed to explode when opened. His appearance aroused the suspicion of the security detail at Ben-Gurion Airport and a young security officer, a woman, ordered him to accompany her to one of the search cubicles. When Hausmann unlocked and opened the valise it exploded, and both of them were killed on the spot.

A British journalist, Ronald Payne, said in a B.B.C. interview that it was highly likely that the blonde German woman in the Air France hijack gang was the same blonde who took part with 'Carlos' in the abduction of the O.P.E.C. ministers in Vienna. Her name as then given was Krocher-Tidman. During the attack on O.P.E.C. headquarters she cold-bloodedly murdered two men, security aides, and told 'Carlos' triumphantly, 'I killed two of them'. At all events, a well-informed official source in Tel Aviv when asked to identify the German terrorist woman answered that it still had not been definitely established.

The identity of only one of the two Arabs involved in the hijacking is known, Ja'il el-Arja, aged thirty-four, who represented the Popular Front for the Liberation of Palestine (P.F.L.P.) in South America and was apparently the liaison between 'Carlos', a presumed Argentine national, and the Front. El-Arja was not a combatant at all and, until the hijacking of the Air France plane, had been engaged primarily in political activity. The French air-bus hijacking was his first operation.

The voice of the German male terrorist crackled out over the loudspeakers ranged along the length of the plane. Speaking with great self-confidence, he read out an announcement on behalf of the Palestine Liberation Movement. It stated that the hijack operation was in reprisal for Zionist 'crimes' in occupied Palestine and the whole world, and as a punishment for France which was an enemy of the Arab people. The announcement came as a surprise, as it had been known that France was pursuing a pro-Arab policy and that terrorist organizations abstained from harming its aircraft.

In the course of the statement the 'captain' declared, 'France sold Mirage planes to Israel and co-operates with the Israel intelligence agencies, and helped Israel to build an atomic bomb'.

The amplifiers went on giving terrorist announcements. 'We're now flying to Benghazi, in Libya. Obey all orders.'

The children on the aircraft did indeed obey the instructions. They sat quietly, almost numbly. Compared with their downcast silence, hysterical outbursts came from some of the adults: 'They're waiting at Benghazi to slaughter us. It will be our end'.

Sarah Davidson hugged her children and tried to pacify them. 'The terrorists don't want to die, either. They'll land the plane safely. The world will get to know about it. They'll start acting to release us. Keep calm . . .'

The conduct of the German female hijacker hardly contributed to assuaging the general anxiety. Once or twice she even 'lost her cool' in a fit of temper. She spun off the skullcap worn by an Orthodox Jewish passenger and screeched, 'I'm tired of your religious superstitions!'

The German 'captain', Boese, perambulated among the rows and continued to apologize that the flight was taking so long. He promised that the plane would soon land at Benghazi and that the passengers would have a meal and a rest. All, he said, on condition that they behaved well and continued to be good.

One of the passengers murmured to her husband that he was like a kindergarten teacher with infants. Rina Cooper's opinion was that the German was comforting himself in true Nazi style. This method was designed first to dissipate every scrap of self-confidence in the victim, take away his weapons, papers and passport, render him defenceless, and then to lull the will to resist by arousing false hopes, to which he clung for want of an alternative.

The most grotesque encounters occurred in almost unbelievable situations. Beside Rina Cooper sat a corpulent man who, despite his greenish eyes, looked like an Arab. He had boarded the aircraft in Athens. From time-to-time, in the most tense and nerve-racking moments, he burst out into laughter. After the plane was hijacked he opened out a map and pored over it.

After a while Rina plucked up courage and asked him where they were at that moment. When he answered his accent left no doubt at all in her mind that he was an Arab. He told her that he lived in Amman, Jordan, and was studying in Philadelphia, in the United States. He even added details about his wife and said she was expecting a child, and had refused to fly.

A conversation developed. Ultimately Rina said to him, 'Look, here are you and I talking together like two human beings, and we're getting on well. Why shouldn't that be the case with our two countries?' The Arab replied that, in his opinion, *this* was the time for peace and that there was an intellectual class in Israel which could help the Arab peoples. Nevertheless, Rina refrained from allowing their colloquy to glide off into political matters. Instead, they talked about themselves. She said, 'Soon they'll kill us because we're Jews and they'll leave you alive'. The peace-loving Arab found time to say, 'You oughtn't to speak like that', when the terrorists separated them.

The first actual news of the fate of the hijacked aircraft came from a pilot of 'Tarum', the Rumanian national airlines, who heard the captain of the seized French airliner request permission to land the aeroplane, named 'Haifa', at Benghazi Airport in Libya.

This report was at once transmitted to the Israeli Prime Minister, Itzhak Rabin. The Government was still immersed in its regular weekly session. Among the subjects on the agenda for discussion was the unauthorized settlement by a group of Jewish religious devotees at a spot called Kaddum in the province of Samaria, on the West Bank of the Jordan river.

The moment the news was given to him the Prime Minister again halted the meeting and told his fellow-ministers of what he knew about the intention of the hijackers to land the aircraft at Benghazi. Before the Cabinet dispersed at 4.15 in the afternoon, the Prime Minister asked five of the ministers to remain behind for further consultations.

The long table in the Cabinet meeting-chamber was now occupied, in addition to the Prime Minister, by the Minister of Defence, Shimon Peres, the Foreign Minister, Yigal Allon, the Minister of Transport, Gad Ya'acobi, the Minister of Justice, Haim Zadok and the Minister without Portfolio, Yisrael Galili. With them were senior government aides, the Director-General of the Prime Minister's office, Amos Eran, and the Director-General of the Ministry for Foreign Affairs, Professor Shlomo Avineri.

After a brief exchange on the subject of the captured airliner, it was decided to distribute assignments to each of those present. The Foreign Minister was deputed to get in touch with his French opposite number at the Quai d'Orsay; Peres was to handle all matters connected with security, and Ya'acobi was to deal with a number of things – to contact the International Civil Aviation Organization (I.C.A.O.) in Montreal, Canada, to give messages to the families of the Israeli captives, and to serve as liaison with the communications media in the state. He was to ensure that no report be published from Israeli sources without the approval of the Foreign and Transport ministries. A complete blackout was also imposed on publication of the names of the Israelis on board the aircraft.

During his telephone conversation with the French Foreign Minister, M. Jean Sauvernagues, Yigal Allon declared that it was the responsibility of France to assure the safety of the passengers on the captured aircraft of the French national airlines company. France replied in the affirmative. She did not try to evade responsibility.

At 9.55 in the evening a message was received to the effect that the hijacked plane had taken off from Benghazi and was flying in the direction of Khartoum, capital of the

Sudan. It was only at 1.45 after midnight, now Monday, 28 June, that news came, clarifying the destination of the plane as Kampala, in Uganda.

Finally at four o'clock in the morning it was learned that the French air-bus had landed at Entebbe, at the north-western tip of Lake Victoria and slightly south of Kampala, capital of Uganda.

It was patently clear that the situation had assumed grave proportions. The only light that shone out in the darkness of uncertainty was the attitude of the French Government and the assurances it had given (apparently with the approval of President Giscard d'Estaing) that France would not abandon the Israelis, and that all the passengers would, without distinction between their origins, 'enjoy everything granted to those protected by the flag of France'.

That same day the Israeli Minister of Tourism, Moshe Kol, stated over the Israel Broadcasting Services that he assumed the Government of France would do all in its power to secure the release of the aircraft with all its passengers, and that it was the concern of the French Government to prevent the innocent from suffering. He went on to ask in his broadcast talk, 'The French are at peace with the Arabs – how then is it possible that it was actually a French aircraft which was hijacked?'

The Israel Television correspondent in Paris, Nakdimon Rogel, reported that several days earlier he had been informed by a French security police aide that it was feared that an Air France plane might shortly be hijacked at Algerian instigation. The same source was of the opinion that the captured aircraft would be landed in an area held by the 'Polisario Front' as a means of drawing world attention to the problem of the Spanish Sahara and the tripartite dispute between Morocco, Algeria and Mauritania, with Spain on the sidelines.

In spite of the mystery that still shrouds the circumstances preceding the actual hijacking, there is common acceptance by public opinion in Israel and the world at large of the view that the operation would not have been possible were it not for the abysmal negligence of security measures at Athens Airport.

More than any other airport in Europe, Athens is known to be the happy hunting ground of Arab terrorists gunning for Israeli aircraft, or passenger-planes on their way to, or from, Israel. So far seven people have been killed and over sixty wounded by terrorist hits at Athens Airport, and even in those instances where the gunmen have been arrested by the Greek authorities, the Arab terror organizations have found the way to effect their speedy release.

The first attack, on Boxing Day, 26 December 1968, had an El Al plane as its target. Two hit-men fired at a defenceless civilian aircraft, killed a Haifa citizen named Leon Shirdan and wounded air stewardess Hannah Shapiro. Both assailants were caught by Greek security police, but it took the juridical authorities in Greece fifteen months to bring them to trial. They were sentenced to fourteen and seventeen years in jail respectively.

On 22 July 1970, six gunmen overpowered an aircraft of the Olympic national airlines of Greece while it was flying over the island of Rhodes in the eastern Mediterranean and forced the pilot to land at Athens. Negotiations began with the Greek Government, which eventually acceded totally to the terrorist demands and freed seven terrorists serving jail terms in Greece, including the two murderers of Leon Shirdan.

One of the most savage attacks ever to have taken place occurred at Athens Airport on 5 August 1973. Although actually meant to sow murder among passengers on an El Al plane, the assault was misdirected and by error the Arab gunmen caused fatalities to dozens of passengers waiting for

15

a T.W.A. plane to take off for Ben-Gurion Airport at Lod, in Israel.

It was a grim harvest of blood – five killed and forty-eight wounded. Two terrorists were caught, tried and sentenced to death. The day they were condemned, Greek Government officials were brazen enough to declare to a correspondent of the Swiss daily *Neue Zuercher Zeitung* that their government reserved its right to pardon the criminals and set them free – this in order not to impair the friendship of their country with Arab states, and prevent a crisis with 'Palestinian guerrilla groups'. Indeed, hardly four months elapsed when the two convicts, members of the 'Popular Front for the Liberation of Palestine', were released and sent to Libya on an Air France plane.

Over the span of nine years, in which Israeli aircraft were a target of Arab terror, the airport at Athens was the most vulnerable because least protected in Europe. As a result of the tragedies there, security measures were augmented and metal-detection devices were installed to search both cargoes and passengers. Greek guards began conducting body and baggage searches of passengers.

Nonetheless, Israeli passengers frequently complained that armed security men were practically invisible in both terminal halls at the airport, in stark contrast to other European airports where armed guards are posted alongside every plane, and special watch is kept over aircraft arriving from, or flying to, Israel.

The Greeks place their faith in electronic facilities which consist of an instrument to scan passenger hand-baggage and an electronic appliance to detect metal objects carried on the person. But this equipment is of course only effective so long as it is not by-passed. Such by-passing and avoidance of detection are common at Athens, where people pass to and fro freely between the open part of the passenger hall and the closed area without anyone paying the least attention.

16

An Israeli passenger who passed through Athens declared: 'Had the terrorists wanted to take aboard the plane two Lance missiles and an armoured troop carrier, they could have done so without any difficulty. The only counter-action by the Greek aviation people would perhaps have been to ask them to pay excess baggage charges'.

In spite of these security drawbacks, Athens Airport is a hive of activity with passengers in-coming and out-going. The geographical location of the city makes it an ideal air traffic junction for planes criss-crossing the eastern basin of the Mediterranean Sea. Distances can be covered in short time – Athens to Lod takes one hour and forty minutes, Cairo to Athens about two hours, and from Beirut one hour and ten minutes.

The day on which Air France plane, Flight 139, stopped over at Athens Airport the security officers were very over-worked, both on account of the great congestion in the terminal halls and a strike among civil aviation employees.

(Some surmises after the hijacking held that the strike had not been caused by strictly professional reasons; certain Arab quarters, it was hinted, were interested to ensure that Athens Airport be a scene of chaos on the day appointed for the snatch. These suppositions were not a figment of the imagination. It was known that extremist Greek movements and even left-wing parties in that country maintained ties with the terrorists and received financial support from them.)

The considerable ease with which the terrorists were able to smuggle their weapons into the Air France liner may be readily understood against this backcloth of malfunction. According to information from a highly reliable Israeli source, the terrorists landed at seven o'clock that same morning from a Singapore Airways plane that had arrived from Kuwait after a stop-over at Bahrein.

17

Contrary to the assumptions after the hijacking that they had received their weapons at Athens, the revolvers, grenades and explosives were already in their hand-baggage when they sat comfortably relaxed in the transit passengers' hall waiting for their Air France plane connection from Israel.

Sarah Davidson hoped in her heart that the French captain, who had the wheel of the aircraft in his hands, would manage in some way or another to delude the hijackers and land the air-bus in a friendly airport. Her hopes were shattered on the rock of reality some minutes before three o'clock that afternoon when a shoreline with a lido-type resort came into sight below against the background of a bistre-hued desert, relieved only by a small landing-strip. It was evident that they had arrived at Benghazi.

Several days later Sarah was to get a reply to her perplexity and vanished hopes. During a conversation that developed with the German hijacker, Boese, in the terminal hall that served as their detention house at Entebbe, she asked him: 'When you were at Athens, how did you know that the pilot would really fly us to Benghazi? After all, he could have pretended that he was obeying your orders and then flown the plane back to Lod or anywhere else'.

Boese looked at her quizzically, smiled and said: 'I learned the subject thoroughly in hijacking drills I took part in in several Arab countries. For months on end I learned how to "read" air maps and to remember all aircraft timings and get acquainted with air-courses. I've got a good grasp of it', the terrorist went on boastfully. 'I knew enough when we "jumped" the plane you were in to know where the captain was flying it and to be sure he was going to Benghazi'.

2 Interlude in Benghazi

The captain circled the field several times and finally made a safe landing on a runway that was new to him. The terrorist leader confirmed to the passengers that they were parked at Benghazi.

The wait was protracted. The burning desert sun beat down mercilessly on the bright metal plate of the aircraft body and the passenger cabin gradually turned into a furnace.

The hijackers had placed in the left-hand doorway of the aircraft a round box with a threatening fuse coiling out of it. Another box, a square one, was attached to the right-hand door.

One of the terrorists, wearing a yellow shirt, said that both doors were booby-trapped with explosives to prevent strangers from coming aboard. But the doors were opened about two hours later and one of the passengers, thirty-year-old Patricia Hyman, of British nationality, was taken off. Mrs Hyman had told her captors that she was in the sixth month of pregnancy and that she had begun bleeding. They allowed her off the craft and released her.

Meanwhile, the plane, which was surrounded by Libyan soldiers, was being re-fuelled. A cold supper was served to the captives at 7.15 in the evening. The stewards passed up and down the plane offering small cartons of juice which were inscribed in Arabic. The atmosphere inside the cabin was relaxed. The passengers gazed out of the windows but all they could see was wilderness and a number of bored soldiers lounging on the tarmac around the plane.

Some distance away three fire-engines were parked.

Doubt assailed some of the trapped travellers. Was this the last halt, here in Libya, under the sway of Colonel Mu'ammar Ghaddafy, who cherished a pathological hatred for the Jewish State? And if they were going to fly off from here, where to? And what were the terrorists' demands?

Boese and his German female confederate were in charge of public order inside the cabin. Anyone wanting to use the toilet had to put up his or her hand, as in class, and a sharp cry would convey consent. When, unwittingly, two passengers rose and went towards the comfort rooms simultaneously without prior notice, the irate voice of the woman rose in almost a bestial roar.

At 7.25 the pseudo-'captain' announced that they would leave in a short while for an unnamed destination and that the flight would take three hours.

An hour later his voice came over the amplifying system, this time to apologize for the delay and the discomfort being caused to the passengers. He promised that they would leave at the earliest possible opportunity. It seemed to some of the captives that the terrorist was trying to play the role of representative of a commercial airline company showing deep concern for the travellers and trying to lift their spirits.

Ten minutes later he again expressed regret, thanking the 'sitting ducks', helpless in their seats, for their patience and good behaviour. In the same breath he urged them to continue to behave quietly.

When the first message reached Paris announcing the captured plane had landed at Benghazi, Jean-Pierre Cabou, French Ambassador at Tripoli, capital of Libya, was ordered to establish immediate contact with the appropriate authorities in order to obtain the release of the aircraft with all its passengers. Proof of this is to be found in the fact that the hijackers had ordered Captain Michel Bacos to prepare for a flight of 3,600 kilometres – the distance between Benghazi and Entebbe.

A short while later the sources in Paris proclaimed that the Ambassador was in close touch with the French Foreign Ministry and that the Libyan authorities had initiated negotiations with the hijackers over their terms for releasing the captives.

But actually the terrorists were in no way interested in negotiating, and their whole purpose was to re-fuel and proceed onwards to the destination on which they had apparently decided in advance.

That same evening the Popular Front for the Liberation of Palestine bragged in a statement that the plane had been seized by men of its 'Special Missions Unit'. An unknown person telephoning from Damascus to the offices of Reuters news-agency in Kuwait gave the information but declined to specify the reasons for the snatch of the plane.

Another phone-call from Kuwait claimed that General (Reserves) Ariel Sharon of the Israeli Army was aboard the captured Air France plane which was then still parked on the airfield at Benghazi. The Kuwaiti newspaper which reported this stated that '... if, indeed, it transpires that "Arik" Sharon is among the passengers, the Popular Front for the Liberation of Palestine intends to put him on trial'.

Upon the news-item appearing in the Israeli daily papers, a number of reporters got in touch with Sharon's farmstead and learned from his family that 'Arik' was in Israel safe and sound.

At 9.35 at night the aircraft took to the air after six-and-a-half hours on the ground. But now worrying questions nagged at the minds of the passengers. Where were they being taken? To Damascus? To Khartoum? To Beirut? Or, maybe, who knew, to Tel Aviv or Paris?

It was very cold inside the cabin. Some covered themselves in blankets, others warmed their limbs with a swathe

21

of newspapers. Sarah Davidson was afraid that the fatigue of the pilots might offer hazards. They were probably tense and worn out, she said to herself, and the job they had was fraught with difficulty and hardship.

Sarah's younger son, Bennie, was asleep on the floor. Most of the passengers dozed in their seats. It was a kind of escape from reality into the arms of Orpheus.

Five hours dragged by and the aircraft still droned under the dark skies. Wakeful passengers were seized by dread. They feared that no airport would permit the plane to land. If the fuel ran out in the tanks before they found a landing place they might plummet to the earth like a mass of metal.

It was now 3.15 in the morning on Monday, 28 June. 'Captain' Boese announced that the aircraft was about to come down at Entebbe, in Uganda. He commanded the passengers to pull down the blinds over the windows and not to look outside.

A few moments later the German terrorist woman proclaimed: 'We're over Uganda. Everything will be all right now, because the airfield is surrounded by Ugandan soldiers'.

That was the first intimation of the conspiracy which had been woven for some time between the ruler of Uganda, Idi Amin Dada, and the terrorist gangs concerning the capture of a plane and its forcible transfer to Entebbe.

Unlike Benghazi, where the plane had to circle over the airfield a long time before being permitted to descend, it was not necessary to wait even one minute for the requisite landing approval at Entebbe Airport. It was a soft and smooth landing.

Before the wheels of the plane came to a halt on the runway the hijackers were glued to the port-hole windows, exchanging glad waves of hands with a number of people of Arab appearance, who obviously had been expecting the aircraft.

The behaviour of the hijackers changed from one extreme to another. Instead of the strict military discipline they had exacted during the first phase of the operation, they now became completely relaxed and it was evident they knew they were in the territory of an ally.

The minds of some of the travellers toyed with the thought: 'We're now in Uganda, the country which was once offered by the British Government for Jewish settlement as a substitute for the Land of Israel. Now it is in the claws of an uninhibited despot known for his hatred of Israel. Will it be our turn to be numbered among his victims?'

Sarah Davidson recorded in her diary:

'I am certain that the Israelis will be separated from the other passengers, because we're going to have another fate. Will they separate families too? Take my husband away from my children and myself? We'll never be able to stand it!

But nonetheless the landing gives you a strange feeling. You get a sort of sense of relief. Earth. It seems less dangerous than to fly through the air with a band of hijackers pointing revolvers at the heads of the pilots. You grant yourself some moments of flight from reality.'

More in the diary:

'Night. Darkness. We're still inside the plane. The "captain" demands that we hand over our documents. Warns that it will go ill for anyone found with documents not handed over. Demands that everything be thrown into a plastic bag.

It's forbidden to go to the comfort rooms except by permission of the hijackers and they escort everyone needing the services. Close-up supervision. The plane is starting to stink.

It's unbearable any longer . . . it's unbearable . . .'

Moshe Peretz lifted the window-blind a little and saw it was daylight. The time was six o'clock in the morning and he wrote in his diary:

'I discerned that we were on a runway on the shore of a

23

tremendous lake. A large number of soldiers lolled in the high grass around the runway. I spoke in Arabic to the one wearing a yellow shirt and he told me that we were likely to stay here a long time. He told me that he had been born in Haifa.

6.20. The "captain" thanks the passengers courteously for the great patience they have shown and announces that negotiations are proceeding with the Ugandan authorities. Idi Amin is going to come himself to announce his decision. One gets the impression that all is going to end well here. The stewards hand out fruit juice to the children and soda to the adults.

8.00. The "captain" says there is nothing to worry about and all is going well. "We shall be given later" he said, "a detailed explanation of the circumstances in which the plane was overpowered." He wished us a pleasant breakfast and added jokingly that it was undoubtedly the first breakfast in our lives in Uganda.'

Breakfast was brought on board by the manager of Entebbe Airport in person. During a conversation that started up between a group of passengers and himself, he said that he had expected 260 travellers and had ordered breakfast for that number.

It was now evident beyond any scintilla of doubt to the captives that their flight to Uganda was not a matter of chance but had been planned in advance with its authorities. The Ugandan breakfast consisted of fried eggs, with black mushrooms and dark meat. The passengers tasted the food and sipped the steaming black coffee.

Now, in the bright light of morning, everything looked less frightening. The 'captain' continued his series of reassuring statements over the loudspeakers:

'Don't worry. No harm will come to you. You probably know that the history of aircraft hijackings has shown that none of the captives have ever been killed.

We'll conduct negotiations. We have claims. If our claims are accepted, we shall release you and send you back soon to your homes and families.'

24

But the German had distorted the history of hijackings: on 21 November 1974, four Palestinian terrorists had hijacked a British Airways VC10 passenger aircraft with forty-seven people on board, and when parked at the airport in the remote kingdom of Dubai had demanded the release of thirteen of their comrades jailed in various places. To show they were serious in their intentions, they dragged out one of their hostages, a middle-aged German banker, told him to kneel, shot him in the back of the head and threw his body out of the doorway to the ground below.

The hostages seized at the straws of hope flung at them, finding solace in them. They said to themselves: 'Look, the "captain" himself is calmer now, and the other hijackers are smiling as if they feel they've come home ...' The back door of the aircraft was wide open and no one stood guard. The terrorists had strung a rope over the gap, knotted out of the stewards' ties.

Time dragged on. Then, suddenly, the hostages discerned the gigantic, heavy-set figure of Idi Amin Dada chatting vivaciously with the men of Arab appearance, who had been awaiting the plane, and Ugandan Officers. The scene was embellished by huggings and kissings amid a general air of triumph and jubilation. Big Daddy had spent a disturbed, sleepless night. He had jumped out of bed at three o'clock, before dawn, dressed and paced to-and-fro in tense anticipation of the arrival of the hijacked aircraft.

Five minutes after the midday hour, the hostages learned from their captors that they were about to be transferred by buses from the aircraft to the terminal building. But within a few moments they changed their minds and ordered the 'captain' to bring the air-bus to the terminal under its own power. The taxi-ing to a spot outside the low building took about five minutes and finally the air-bus ground to a halt outside that old, dilapidated structure.

The passengers descended from the aircraft with a feeling

of deep relief after their prolonged ordeal in the air. Three of the hijackers stood in the doorway of the plane. As they came down on to the tarmac, the weary travellers passed between two lines of frozen-faced Ugandan soldiers who pointed rifles at them.

The air-pirates, looking pleased and self-satisfied, followed on at the rear of the column of passengers. Several of the latter waved their hands at the terrorists to signify 'good-bye'. They evidently believed this had ended the chapter as far as the plane-snatchers were concerned. The fact that they had been allowed to leave the aircraft and go into the civilian airport terminal presumably 'proved' that there had been negotiations which were successful, and now, they hoped, they would be transferred to other civilian aircraft to fly to Paris.

The hostages gathered in clusters inside the building, which consisted of nothing more than a large, filthy hall, where thick layers of dust cloaked everything in sight, indicating that the place had been out of use for many months.

Some of the passengers sprawled in the dusty armchairs and Ugandan soldiers hauled in more chairs from elsewhere. The passengers still held on to their hand-bags, and some of them began enquiring when the porters would bring their baggage from the hold of the aircraft . . .

3 Mine Host Idi Amin

Contrasting with the hopeful belief of those hostages who thought negotiations had already been successfully concluded, the fact of the matter was that contacts had not even been initiated. Indeed, everyone in Israel and elsewhere were entirely in the dark as to the terrorists' demands.

The President of France had consented to handle the matter of the captured plane – this, in his own words, out of 'humanitarian reasons' – and confused (and confusing) reports on contacts between France, Uganda and the terrorists came hard on the heels of each other.

The French Ambassador at Kampala, Pierre Renard, arrived at the focus of events on the Entebbe airfield immediately after the aircraft had landed and negotiated with the hijackers for fourteen hours under the broiling African sun. Finally he returned to the Ugandan capital which lay thirty-two kilometres north-east of the airfield. He refused to talk to newsmen, but a French Embassy spokesman at Kampala stated that the talks with the hijackers had been fruitless and even were at a stalemate.

'We still don't know what the hijackers want', the spokesman said, 'and until we do, there's little that can be done.'

It was the French Ambassador who disclosed to the outside world the report that the hostages had left the plane and were being held in the terminal building.

The demands being made by the terrorists were to be revealed only twenty-four hours later, and although their substance was foreseen, they were astounding in their scope.

They insisted in return for the release of the hostages and

27

the aircraft on the freeing of fifty-three 'freedom fighters' held in jails in Israel, France, West Germany, Switzerland and Kenya. In addition to Arabs, convicted persons of other nationalities were on the list.

The hijackers declared their demands to be a 'final ultimatum' – fifty-three jailed terrorists to be flown from the countries in which they were imprisoned to Entebbe Airport – until two o'clock on Thursday afternoon. They chose to bring their demands to the notice of the Government of France through the President of Uganda, Idi Amin Dada.

The demands consisted of five clauses:

First: all the fifty-three persons named in the list were to be flown by special plane to Entebbe, and this craft would be used to fly out the hijackers.

Second: Air France to be responsible for flying to Entebbe those who were jailed in Israel. It would have to check that the freed prisoners were actually on the plane together with the aircrew, 'and no one else'.

Third: the other countries would have to make their own arrangements to fly the released terrorists to Uganda.

Fourth: the representatives of the P.F.L.P. in the talks with the French Government would be Hashi Abdallah, Somali Ambassador in Kampala. The hijackers were not prepared to recognize anyone else except him.

Fifth: France must appoint a special envoy to conduct negotiations with the hijackers.

Unless these conditions were met in full by the deadline on Thursday, the group threatened savage reprisals. In an interview with a foreign correspondent, a Ugandan officer said that, in his opinion, the guerrillas were only pretending and they had no intention of blowing up the building with all its occupants. But even he agreed with the reporter that the difference between 'impression' and 'execution' in this case was a very slender one when it came to uninhibited terrorists.

The latter themselves made it clear that they would not rest content with a mere agreement by the countries concerned to release their comrades, and demanded that they all be brought to Entebbe before the ultimatum expired.

That same day, Tuesday, 29 June, the Government of Israel had received prior word that the terrorists were about to present their demands. In anticipation of this possibility the Prime Minister, Itzhak Rabin, called together a special team of Ministers to an afternoon conference.

But the clock ticked on by the second, the minute, the hour, and no authentic report of the demands came to hand. Twenty minutes before the meeting was due to open at four o'clock, the telephone rang on the desk of Professor Shlomo Avineri, Director-General of the Foreign Ministry in Jerusalem. Mordecai Gazit, Israel's Ambassador in France, was on the line with particulars of the demands.

Time was pressing, and instead of sending the terrorist demands over the teleprinter, as was the practice, Gazit used the telephone and Avineri jotted down the long list of names which the Ambassador in Paris dictated. Then he rushed them to the conference room where the team of ministers was in session.

Several names stood out on the list of convicted terrorists whom Israel was commanded to release:

Archbishop Hilarion Capucci, who had been spiritual leader of the Greek Catholic community in East Jerusalem, and was sentenced to seven years' imprisonment for smuggling arms from Arab states to terrorists in Israel in his luxury car, which enjoyed diplomatic immunity. Capucci had been active in the service of the El Fatah organisation.

Kozo Okamoto, a member of the Japanese terror gang known as the 'Red Army', who had been one of the trio spraying death and disaster at Tel Aviv's Ben-Gurion Airport – 'the night of the blood-bath' – at the end of May

1972. Okamoto had been sentenced to life imprisonment for his share in the massacre, in which twenty-four peaceful citizens, many of whom were Puerto Rican pilgrims to the holy places in Israel, had been killed, and scores wounded.

Fatmeh Baranawy, a swarthy Arab woman, resident of Jerusalem, convicted of placing explosives in the Zion Cinema in central Jerusalem in 1968 and sentenced to life imprisonment.

William George Nasser, one of the first to join the El Fatah organization, who was detained in East Jerusalem in 1968 and given a life term for acts of sabotage and murder, including that of a Druse watchman at a work-site outside Jerusalem.

Even after receipt of the terrorists' terms the Israel Government did not swerve from its standpoint in principle, and informed the French Government that it was held to be primarily responsible for the fate of the hostages. The Foreign Ministry in Jerusalem immediately communicated with the other countries which had been served with an ultimatum to free convicted terrorists – Germany, Switzerland and Kenya.

On the day on which the demands had been made known, most of the European Foreign Ministers were at a session of the Ministerial Council of the European Community being held in Luxembourg. Their agenda was crowded with matters of European domestic concern, but they broke off at once to deal with the hijacking of the Air France air-bus.

The French Foreign Minister informed reporters that France 'definitely rejected the unreasonable demands of the hijackers'. The press representatives were somewhat sceptical about this statement which M. Jean de Sauvenargues made with such firmness. They were more inclined to suspect the French tendency to give undue consideration to Arab positions.

But one point was clear to all, and that was that the attitude of the European governments which were commanded to release terrorists would be largely dependent on the position taken by the Government of Israel. The Bonn authorities in West Germany took the lead in the formation of a common front among the governments concerned.

It was not the first time that the domain of international civil aviation had been rocked by the overpowering of a civilian aircraft carrying passengers of various nationalities, and making their release conditional on setting at large convicted terrorists from jails in Israel or other countries.

Nor was the freeing of seven terrorists by the Greek Government in July 1970 in exchange for a captured Olympic Airways plane, as already mentioned, a lone instance of surrender to extortion under duress.

Four aircraft belonging to Swissair, T.W.A., B.O.A.C. and Pan-American, which had been hijacked in September 1970 and blown up on the ground at an out-of-the-way desert runway in the kingdom of Jordan, accounted for another major blow at the world's civilian airlines. Only the submission of the governments of Germany, Switzerland and Great Britain for the release of terrorists had saved the lives of hundreds of captive passengers taken off before the four aeroplanes were wantonly destroyed by explosives.

A particularly revolting incident was the release of the murderers of eleven Israeli sportsmen who had been trapped in the Olympic Games at Munich in 1972 following the hijacking of a Lufthansa aircraft.

The Israeli Government had also to give in to blackmail on two occasions when Israeli citizens were held by terrorists. The first was in July 1968. An El Al plane had been hijacked over Italy, and the pilot forced to change course and land in Algeria. Prolonged and exhausting negotiations through the Italian Government led to the release of the plane and its passengers six weeks later in return for what was termed 'a humanitarian gesture by Israel towards Italy', namely, the freeing of sixteen terrorists from Israeli jails.

The second occasion was at the end of August 1969. Terrorists overcame a T.W.A. plane and force-landed it at Damascus Airport. The passengers were freed with only two exceptions – both Israeli citizens. The two were imprisoned by the Syrian authorities and released only three months later as a ransom for thirteen Syrian prisoners, including two military pilots who had been in captivity in Israel.

A third instance of surrender to terrorists was unconnected with aircraft. El Fatah terrorists, who crossed over from the Lebanon at the end of December 1969, captured a village watchman named Samuel Rosenwasser in the fields of Metullah, a Jewish settlement on the northern frontier. He was detained and returned only two months later through the Red Cross in exchange for a terrorist named Mahmoud Hijazi, who had been serving a thirty-year sentence for sabotage in an Israeli prison.

Israel had made supreme efforts for many years not to release terrorists in exchange for hostages. It stuck to this policy of 'no surrender' even when a heavy price had to be paid, as in the tragic affair at Ma'alot, a village on the northern frontier, when, during the first moments of an assault by Israeli army units designed to free the hostages, the terrorists managed to kill twenty-six hostages, mostly school children.

An outstanding exemplar of this aspect of the Israeli Government's policy was the hijacking of a Sabena aircraft while *en route* from Brussels to Tel Aviv in May 1972. The Boeing 707 was overpowered by two male and two female terrorists, members of the 'Black September' gang – named for the month in which the Jordanian Government had taken counter-measures against the terrorist organization in that kingdom and smashed it to smithereens with considerable loss of life to its members.

The Sabena aeroplane was carrying ninety passengers and

ten aircrew members. The hijackers forced the captain to land at Lod airport and their leader demanded the release of most of the terrorists then imprisoned in Israel, who totalled three hundred and seventeen.

Negotiations with the terrorist chieftain, who introduced himself as Kamal Rifa'at, were conducted from the control tower by Major-General Aharon Yariv, now in the reserves and a member of the Israel 'Knesset' (parliament). Beside him in the wide-windowed tower room were the Ministers of Transport and Defence, the Chief of Staff and several army generals.

During the night, under cover of darkness, while the captive passengers, the crew and hijackers were asleep and in low-profile vigilance, Israeli security men crept up to the aircraft which was parked on a side runway near a verge of high grass, and let the air out of the tyres.

Then, the next morning, the negotiators on the Israeli side ostensibly acceded to the terrorist demands, and the latter agreed to let a group of mechanics come up to prepare the plane for a take-off.

The 'mechanics' belonged to an élite combat unit, who had been clad in the white overalls of the type used by aircraft engineers. Within minutes the commandos burst into the main cabin through the emergency exits and shot and killed the two male hijackers. The women were spared, though one of them was badly wounded, and in the exchange of fire an Israeli woman passenger was fatally injured. It was later ascertained that the leader of the hijacking squad was Ali Abu Sneina, a well-known terrorist, who had also taken part in the capture of the El Al plane force-landed in Algeria and a Lufthansa plane made to fly to Aden.

The sorties by the Palestinian terror groups which had for years been directed against targets inside Israel alone over-spilled from 1968 onwards to other countries.

33

Beginning in July 1968, when the El Al aircraft was bumped into Algeria, and until the snatch of the Air France air-bus at Athens, almost eight years later, no less than two hundred-and-one men and women paid with their lives in these criminal acts and two hundred-and-thirteen were wounded. The total number of such incidents was one hundred-and-fifty-three.

Twenty-nine acts of hijacking and hits at aircraft were perpetrated in these years, three attacks at different airports and eleven attempted hijackings or assaults which were foiled. The peak year for terrorist swoops against Israeli targets overseas was in 1973, when fifty attempts were made, including a number at other than Israeli places.

Terrorist acts were carried out in thirty-nine countries, most of the 'hits' being committed by the El-Fatah organization – one of its arms, code-named 'Black September'.

It should be noted that, save for the first attempt to hijack an El Al aircraft in 1968, no other terrorist sally against the Israel national airline succeeded in its purpose. The second attempt to snatch an El Al plane in September 1970, during a flight from London to Tel Aviv, resulted in the wounding of the terrorist Leila Khaled. It was frustrated in mid-air by security men with the help of aircrew. It is sad to reflect that few airlines have copied the El Al example in applying appropriate security precautions.

Entebbe. The antiquated terminal hall, measuring twenty by fifteen metres, was jam-packed with two hundred-and-fifty-seven people, women, children and men – passengers and French aircrew. In spite of the stifling atmosphere and the congestion, most of them felt an odd sense of relief. For them the terminal, with all its shortcomings in comfort, was much safer than the booby-trapped metal air-bird sitting on the tarmac outside.

A row of low windows punctuated the façade of the

building looking out at the runway. The other walls were blank. A short corridor led from the main hall to the comfort services rooms. The 'captain' did not leave his involuntary 'guests' alone. He followed them around the hall, speaking to them in his quiet, courteous manner:

'You're now on the soil of Uganda under the control of the forces of the Front for the Liberation of Palestine. You must know that we're negotiating with your governments and hope everything will soon be settled for the best.

As long as you strictly obey our orders, no harm will come to you.'

An hour later an unusual incident occurred, probably without precedent in the annals of aeroplane hijackings. Ugandan soldiers escorted a team of Uganda television personnel into the hall. The place was lit up and the cameras whirred. Everyone tried to push in towards the radius of the lenses in the hope that the film would be shown on television screens in their home countries and their families there would be reassured of their welfare.

The air-pirates, too, posed in front of the cameras, exuding an air of over-weening triumph.

Ugandan servitors brought large tureens heaped high with rice covered with a sharp curry. Many of the passengers were unable to pluck up courage to taste the meat served with the rice. 'Maybe it's crocodile meat', one of them joked. Others refused to drink the water, the murky appearance of which put them off.

The building was ringed by husky Ugandan commando troops with weapons at the ready. The passengers still believed that the hour of their liberation was near and the central issue under discussion was how long it would take to fly from Uganda to Paris. They hoped that, if the plane left at once, they would be in Paris by nightfall, or a short while later.

Sarah Davidson recorded in her diary:

'A plane will shortly arrive to take us. Everything is now being settled. We'll soon be flying onwards, on our family excursion ...

Illusions maybe, because a situation like this makes you want to delude yourself. Maybe the soul needs delusions, to fortify it ...

We're allowed to go to the services. Hours go by – and we're still here. That's the danger of illusions. When they're not fulfilled you get frustrated. We believe we're at the centre of world attention. For sure the whole world holds its breath and is worrying only about our release. But, look, nothing happens. Darkness will soon fall and we're still here. Has the world forgotten us? Doesn't anyone care what is going to happen to us?'

The rumour circulates from lips to ear that Idi Amin will shortly be coming to pay a visit. One of the captives narrated after his release: 'I really felt at that moment what fear meant. Amin was something like Hitler. I felt that I was in a world of frightening nightmare, like the concentration camps of the Second World War'.

Actually most of the captives looked fairly relaxed. One of them gazed out at the waters of Lake Victoria which could be seen as a broad expanse rolling away beyond the windows, and mused: 'I never thought I'd see Lake Victoria in Africa'.

A few minutes later came the clack-clack-clacking whir of a helicopter over the building. Idi Amin made his entrance. Beside his giant figure walked a boy of seven or eight. Both of them, father and son, wore identical army uniform with dozens of glittering medals festooning in rows the father's broad chest repeated in a smaller replica on the uniform of the junior field-marshal.

With their advent the congregation of captives clapped their hands in enthusiastic applause. Was this ovation an expression of gratitude for 'imminent liberation' or perhaps an obeisance before the capricious tyrant?

The ruler of Uganda was in jovial mood. He burst into frequent laughter, revealing rows of gleaming white teeth, shook hands on right and left and kept reiterating time without number: 'Welcome to Uganda, welcome!'

The Israelis at once spotted that the parachute wings adorning his left breast had the emblem of the Defence Army of Israel.

'Big Daddy' stood with his feet planted apart in the centre of the passenger hall, green beret aslant on his head, and proclaimed in a portentous voice: 'Some of you know me and some don't. Well, for those who don't know me, I'm Field-Marshal Dr Amin Dada. I looked after you and arranged that you be allowed to get off the plane and stay in Uganda'.

He went on to say that the terrorists' demands were fair but Israel had nonetheless rejected them out of hand, although the other countries had acceded to them.

At the end of his speech he was once more greeted by a tumult of encouraging cries and hand-clapping by some of the captives. The rest of the hostages found it an astounding spectacle that even aroused their disgust. Idi Amin went out and an 'army' of African women came into the hall, each carrying an armchair on her head. There was sufficient seating for all.

After supper was served at eight o'clock, consisting of meat and potatoes, green beans and small bananas, a Ugandan doctor came and distributed two anti-malaria pills to every passenger. With darkness small worries took the place of the larger anxiety. People started preparing to sleep. Some of them curled up in the armchairs creaking with age, others found a pile of ancient mattresses; but most preferred to lie on the filthy floor in the sweltering heat in which flights and squadrons of great mosquitoes zoomed and swooped and stung the flesh.

The few who had found the mattresses were regaled by

stings and bites of another nature. It appeared that these straw mattresses were the refuge of a dense colony of bugs. But the accumulated fatigue of the preceding forty-eight hours overcame lesser drawbacks and people were soon fast asleep. Heavy snoring arose on all sides.

Among those whose sleep was uneasy was Sarah Davidson. She added a comment to her diary the following morning:

'... It seems funny to me that I didn't want to lie down on a mattress for fear of bugs. I'm ready to "embrace" bugs so long as I have a mattress.'

But her younger son Bennie brought his mother back to the hard ground of reality. He murmured quietly, '*Ima*, we won't get out of here. We won't get out'.

Daylight streaming into the hall through the long line of windows illuminating the frontage revealed to the captives that they were surrounded by Ugandan soldiers. The Ugandan army personnel were posted at a distance of less than twenty yards from the exterior wall of the terminal. It was plain for all to see that the Ugandan soldiery had been ordered to help the abductors to guard their captives.

It was now the turn of the Ugandan army to play a role in the struggle for the liberation of Palestine. The four 'original' air-pirates were now able to enjoy a respite and re-charge their dynamos with renewed energy while their confederates, who had waited for them in Uganda, watched over the captives with loaded pistols and automatic weapons in hand.

The function of the German 'captain' Boese was now assumed by another terrorist, one of the trio who had welcomed the plane and had been permitted to drive in their Mercedes limousines right up to the doors of the aircraft. These cars had been driven by uniformed Ugandan soldiers.

The new leader of the group was Antonio Degas Bouvier, a South American, bearer of an Ecuadorian passport, who had been head of the 'Carlos' ring in London and had vanished after it was uncovered.

Bouvier had tried in December 1973 to murder J. Edward Sieff, one of the leaders of Anglo-Jewry and President of the Marks and Spencer chain of department-stores. Born in Quito, capital of Ecuador, Bouvier had first met up with the legendary 'Carlos' during training exercises in Cuba, where terrorists took special tactical courses under Bouvier's tutelage.

Both of them decided to co-operate with George Habash, chief of the P.F.L.P. in carrying out a series of assaults at Israeli and Jewish targets in Europe. For this purpose they rented two apartments in the West End of London which became the base of their conspiracies. Following the failure of the attempt on 'Teddy' Sieff's life, Bouvier had to flee from London.

Two other terrorists had awaited the arrival of the Air France air-bus but only the identity of one was known. He was Faiz Abdul-Rahim Jaber, aged forty-six, born in Hebron and a resident of that town until 1946, when he moved to Egypt. He married there and had six children. Despite his educational limitations, Faiz was able to rise to a senior post in George Habash's organization, the P.F.L.P. by virtue of the 'revolutionary spirit' animating him.

For years his adventurous activities had been well-known to Israel's security services, which maintained close surveillance over his family home at Hebron in an effort to keep track of him. Four of Faiz Jaber's five brothers were deported by the Israeli authorities after the Six-Day War in June 1967 and the fifth, Rasmi Jaber, still living in Hebron where he runs a souvenir store, was suspected by the Israel security arm of having organized hostile activity and had been detained many times, though never brought to trial through lack of evidence.

The hijackers repeated their statement many times that

they were acting under the inspiration of Habash's organization. But after the Air France aircraft had been taken, George Habash himself, in an interview with the weekly *Monday Morning*, insisted that the snatch had been carried out by 'former members' of his group, who had seceded from it some time ago. He strongly denied that his organization had any connection with the hijacking.

'Anyone can pretend that he belongs to the "Front"', Habash declared, adding, 'The "Front" is represented through a number of central bodies, namely, the Central Committee, the Political Bureau and the Central Command ... Any announcement that does not come from our information H.Q. does not express the position or views of the "Popular Front".'

According to him, his organization had decided four years ago to suspend the hijacking of planes 'because victory over Zionism will be achieved only through armed struggle, like the struggle now going on in the Lebanon'.

If there are grounds to the rumour (originated in a South African publication) that Idi Amin had been ready to take part in another plane hijack (with the largest possible number of American passengers) so that it could be ransomed for one hundred million dollars, to be remitted to the 'Popular Front' for financing its activities, then all of Habash's expostulations and repudiation of any link with the capture of the Air France plane can only arouse doubt, if not more than that. Indeed, there is one thing beyond all doubt – the organizers of the operation were members of the breakaway group of which Dr Wadie Hadad was the leader.

Hadad is the most mysterious figure of all among the terror organizations. Contrary to his associates, who frequently make public appearances in order to be photographed and brag of their deeds, Wadie tries to hide his identity under a bushel of anonymity – and in this respect it should be recalled that the photograph which appeared in hundreds of papers as Hadad's likeness is, according to all indications, the photo of someone else entirely.

Wadie Hadad was born in Safad and lived in Jerusalem for many years. He studied medicine and graduated as a surgeon. Together with George Habash, also a physician by calling, Hadad started a clinic in Amman, capital of Jordan. Both doctors were leaders of the 'Arab Nationalist' movement, which transformed its complexion after the Six-Day War in 1967 and became known as the 'Front for the Liberation of Palestine'.

Wadie Hadad is estimated as the most dangerous person in the terror movement today and all his activities contradict his mission as a medical practitioner devoted to saving human life. Within the 'Front' set-up he served as head of the operational arm and in that capacity planned the most spectacular terror sorties of the 'Front' over the years. His hand was in all the 'hits' outside the borders of Israel, including the attempt on the life of the venerable David Ben-Gurion while he was in Denmark on his way to the United States.

In 1968 Hadad began to engage in aeroplane kidnappings. But in the wake of the massacre by the three Japanese terrorists at Lod Airport in 1972, the first signs became evident of a rift in the relations between Habash and Hadad, as the details of the plan had not received the prior approval of the leader of the P.F.L.P. The murderous character of the operation pointed clearly to the fact that Hadad, who does not recoil from any extreme violent measure or most inhuman act imaginable, was the originator and planner of that St Valentine's night slaughter at Lod.

Later on, Hadad moved his headquarters to Baghdad and set up there the 'Revolutionary Front for the Liberation of Palestine'. He financed its programmes out of the five million dollars received as ransom from the Lufthansa airline for the release of one of its aircraft hijacked by his group and flown to Aden.

Forty-six year old Hadad is a man of handsome appearance, the reason perhaps why he is able to charm the fair sex and use them so frequently to carry out his lethal plots. Among these female aides was Muna Saudi, who was enlisted by him to assassinate David Ben-Gurion. Others included Leila Khaled, who took part in the foiled attempt to hijack an El Al Boeing, and Katie Thomas, who masterminded the snatch of a Japanese airliner and even paid for it with her life. Last but not least, and the most unpleasant of them all, was the blonde female pirate who took part in the Air France plane abduction at Athens.

Consequently, the retiring Dr Wadie Hadad is known to the world only by virtue of his extraordinary savage plotting and acts and his close connection with such world terror underground elements as the 'Red Army', the Baader-Meinhof gang that operates from West Germany, 'Carlos' and clandestine anarchist groups in Turkey and Iran.

These secret contrivings with foreign terror cabals have borne fruit. It was the Baader-Meinhof gang which helped the P.F.L.P. in the fiendish attack on the Israeli sports champions at the Olympic Games in Munich, as testified by a 'Front' spokesman. The 'blood-bath' at Lod airport in May 1972 was perpetrated by terrorists of the Japanese 'Red Army'. These Japanese criminals were trained for their mission first in North Korea and then, in 'specialized courses', in Syria and the Lebanon. The only one of the trio who survived was Kozo Okamoto, now held in an Israeli jail, whose release the French air-bus hijackers had demanded. To underline the scope of complicity within the sphere of international terror it should be mentioned that the requisite funds to finance their action were received by the Japanese in East Germany and their firearms were handed over in Rome, capital of Italy.

A report published by the American Central Intelligence Agency recently disclosed for the first time that the 'Popular Liberation Army in Turkey' was permitted to use a Palestinian camp in Syria for its training exercises and the 'price' exacted for that favour was the murder of the Israeli Consul in Istanbul, Ephraim El-Rom. The same source also reported the growing involvement of Cuban terrorists in operations in Africa and the Middle East. Cuban instructors are training tyros in Syria and the Lebanon, and training centres for Palestinian terrorists are functioning at top speed in Havana, capital of Cuba.

There is no doubt that countries such as Algeria, Libya and lately even Uganda, which afford shelter to terrorists, contribute their not negligible share to the spread of international terror. A characteristic trait of these countries is that all are run by military dictatorships, headed by racist despots whose sanity is open to speculation, to say the least, and who resort to methods of terror and torture in order to maintain their stranglehold over the citizens of their countries.

Another characteristic of these 'lands of lunacy' is their political conspirings in other countries through the use of violence, and trying to undermine their régimes in complete contempt of the rules of international law.

It is an open secret that these rulers receive lavish Soviet aid in the form of financial subventions, arms and political backing in their constant conniving to dislocate law and order in a powerless world. The claim by those who declare that the real wire-pullers of the 'International Terror Syndicate' are none other than the rulers inside the Kremlin cannot therefore be discounted. There are distinct signs showing that the various terror organizations, which ostensibly operate independently in sundry parts of the world and

43

whose aims vary, have developed 'mediators' in the guise of liaison units co-ordinating their operations. It would seem that 'Carlos' is one of these intermediates.

Gil Kessary, a reporter on the Tel Aviv Hebrew afternoon paper *Ma'ariv*, has an interesting theory. He writes:

'There is an assumption that the increase of international terror operations in recent years is the outcome of a secret conference of the "International Terror Syndicate" that took place at the beginning of 1972 in the Badawy refugee camp in the Lebanon with the object of "shocking the world".

It was agreed at that gathering that "each organization will commit acts of sabotage, terror and murder on behalf of another organization in order to cover up the tracks".

Most of the members of the organizations were trained for murder missions and sabotage in the Lebanon, Libya and Cuba. This international ring has a common ideology – revolutionary Marxism. There are indications of co-operation, if not ideological then at least practical, even with Fascist-Nazi circles, especially in Italy and Spain. Arms of the "International Terror" have been set up in these countries under the guise of business firms named "Paladin" which has its head offices in the city of Alicante, in Spain, and is headed by a man who calls himself Dr G. N. von Schubert. This organization published openly its "I Believe" in these terms:

"Hazards do not deter us; we obey orders in the national and international spheres. Everything is carried out in utter secrecy. Experts in actions of all kinds are at our disposal, ready to go anywhere to execute our instructions. All negotiations are kept secret".'

All these associations and militant arms enjoy many sophisticated international connections and means for action, both in finances and firearms. It has long since been made patently clear to the wire-pullers that international terror is also a most profitable enterprise. The development of these different terror-striking forces has more than once been dictated by economic calculations. 'Terror' is big business, in which the investments are minimal and the dividends to be expected enormous. The London weekly *Spectator* has claimed that 'anyone speaking of terror organizations as guerrilla or commando fighters waging a social-underground struggle is about five years behind our times'.

The free world, with its libertarian régimes of limited powers, serves as a convenient ground for the sprouting of international terror. It thus follows that these organizations exploit for their own ends, which are opposed to international law, both the democratic countries and those countries ruled by régimes of tyranny and terror, and all this under the cloak of 'freedom fighters'.

Within this context of international terror the practitioners of Arab terror have an unusual role in that they use peaceful people as hostages for the purposes of blackmail, and do not recoil from the most savage and even barbaric methods. This may be explained by the fact that Arab terrorists find no difficulty in seeking concealment in some sovereign Arab and African countries which grant them free transit and havens of refuge, to which they can return after carrying out their strikes. Moreover, as has already been pointed out, even in those cases where the perpetrators have been caught and imprisoned, they have every good prospect of being freed within a short while by more acts of hijacking and extortion by their confederates in terrorism.

4. Dialogues

The third day of captivity was drawing to a close. Sometime during the evening, as the hostages waited for their meal, the German hijacker came into the hall holding a long list, from which he read out names.

After he had rattled off a few it became evident that they were only Israelis. Moshe Peretz recorded in his diary:

'19.10. The terrorists are separating us from the rest in most dramatic fashion. Everyone with an Israeli passport is asked to go out of the main hall into an adjoining one. There is a sense of imminent execution. Women begin to weep.'

Sarah Davidson, too, wrote with trembling hand in her diary:

'The routine has been broken. The Israelis have been parted from the other passengers. It is clear now that we're not human beings like all the others. We – our fate is different.

The German, none other, entered the hall of detention and in that quiet, reassuring manner of his explained: "We're separating you, but not because of nationality, there's no connection between that and the separation. I'll call out names and whoever hears their names will go into the other room. Really, we're doing this so that you won't be so crowded. It has nothing to do with nationality."

Uzi and Ron and Bennie and I again press together. Yes nationality, no nationality, just so that they won't part us, only that!

And the German stands with that list and begins to read names and "by chance", "quite by chance", he calls out only Israeli names, "without any connection with nationality". And the Israelis – they even "help" him, and rightly so; when the name of an Israeli male is read out, his wife and children at once jump up and insist on going with him into the second hall, and the "good German" smiles and "allows", as though it were his intention in the first place.

All the Israelis – into the second room. But not just like that. Not to go through an ordinary door. *To humiliate.* Between the first hall and the new one – a common wall. A plywood partition has been taken down and a gap made for passage, through which one can pass erect. But the terrorists have put up there a sort of barrier, in the form of the English letter "T" and the open part is very low. An Arab terrorist stands there armed and ready. The German reads the names over a loudspeaker and everyone who hears his name goes to the exit, grinds his teeth and crawls under the "T". The German woman takes over from the Arab as the guard over the new passage. Tough. Wicked. Just give her a chance.

Because of the emotions stirred up by the separation, many of us need the comfort rooms. The German woman has to be asked for permission to go to the services in the former chamber, as there are no toilets in this one.

She smiles venomously and motions at the "T" – crawl, crawl. And so we crawl, there and back.'

Two couples who were not Israeli citizens joined the group of Israelis and those with dual nationality. Both males wore skullcaps and drew the attention of the hijackers while they were still aboard the plane, when they donned *tefillin*, phylacteries, on their foreheads and left bare forearms. A religious Jew deserved, in the estimation of the terrorists, to be counted among the Israeli citizens even if he did not have the passport of 'the Zionist State' in his pocket . . .

There were no armchairs in the new hall, but some kind of old, semi-upholstered benches, seats ripped out of disused aircraft. The Israelis wanted to transfer a number of armchairs and mattresses from the first hall where they had spent the previous night, and their request was granted.

Akiba, a religious young man, wearing a knitted skullcap, organized the distribution of mattresses. Suddenly, for no apparent reason, a moustachio'd terrorist jumped at him and gave him a heavy blow on the neck.

Second night at Entebbe. The passengers are afflicted by another 'Uganda plague' – tiny midges. They penetrate into the ears and eyes. A terrible cry resounds from the nearby hall. A French woman hostage cannot endure the tension any longer and has a nervous breakdown.

Sarah Davidson is afraid that the others too face a similar fate. She writes in her diary:

'I've no strength left. It's even hard to write. I gaze at my children and pray that they'll emerge sound in body and spirit from this nightmare.'

During the day Sarah had conducted prolonged conversations with the German terrorist who was in charge of them. He was an enigma to her. She was aware of the Palestinian viewpoint but found it hard to understand what the German was doing, intellectual and wise as he looked to her, among the Arabs.

When he stood guard over them, she began to talk to him and posed her question. He answered that he believed in the rights of the Palestinian people whose unfortunate sons lacked house and homeland. He could not remain 'indifferent' to their plight, he said, and his wish was to help them.

Sarah pointed out that, as far as could be seen, he was not well-versed in the history of Palestine and ignored the fact that the Palestinian Arabs had been offered a state of their own in the Resolution of the United Nations Organization in November 1947, which had recommended the creation of two states, Arab and Jewish, in the area of Mandated Palestine. The Arabs of the country, with the encouragement of neighbouring Arab states, had rejected the offer and chose to go to war in the hope of wiping out the Jews and taking over the whole of the territory designed to be partitioned.

The blond 'revolutionary' listened with great attention, but it appeared that the presence of his German accomplice, who stood nearby, bothered him. It was obvious that he felt uncomfortable. He kept shooting glances towards her. But Sarah did not give up. She asked him a provocative question. Let's suppose, she said, that the terrorists succeed in their purpose of liquidating Palestine, then the Jews will remain without a motherland of their own. Would you then agree to rush to their assistance? Would you hijack planes for their sake?

The German had an answer, although it stumbled from his lips somewhat confusedly.

'You, the Jews, really need a state of your own', he said, continuing that he was in favour of the existence of Israel. But he also favoured a Palestinian state that should be established alongside Israel, or for the transformation of Israel into a common state for Arabs and Jews. When referring to the Palestinians he continually used the first personal pronoun, 'we'.

'The Arabs after all have so many states', Sarah remarked, 'and the Jews have only one tiny corner in the world'.

The German kept silent.

The conversation took place in the entrance to the hall, near the children who were playing on the grass, and the atmosphere appeared tranquil and outwardly calm. It was the period before the 'selection'. Sarah started to return to the main hall but, to her astonishment, the German said he wanted to continue the conversation, and then fired questions at her. 'Have you ever seen a Palestinian refugee camp? Have you seen how these people live? Have you seen their children?'

Sarah replied, 'If there were more Jewish States in the world apart from Israel, the Jews would have no problem at all settling in them and soon becoming citizens with equal rights, capable of looking after their livelihoods and homes. But how did the Arab countries handle the Palestinian refugees who came into them? These unfortunate people were treated by the Arab rulers as "political weapons" and no more. They didn't absorb them nor gave them rights of citizenship. The Arab countries hadn't the least intention of solving their problems. They dealt with them as inferior citizens and not like their fellow-people'.

The German's face turned pale and showed the signs of deep inner feeling.

'Yes', he blurted out, 'they're all reactionaries – the Egyptians, the Syrians, all of them. They don't care about their own people.'

'There's plenty of room in the Middle East for all the peoples', Sarah added. 'But how can the profound hatred of the Arabs for us be overcome?'

He did not answer her question, probably because he had nothing to say. After a short, thoughtful pause, he said, 'Yes. You have a very lovely country. Very lovely.'

That morning the captives were privileged to have another visit by Idi Amin. In his direct manner he told the people that he had not closed an eye during the night and that he was doing 'everything' for their sake. He had nothing but reproaches for the Government of Israel. It was not responding to the terrorist demands and under such circumstances he was unable to help.

His hands were tied, he said, so long as Israel's acquiescence in the terms put by the abductors was not forthcoming. He had but one request – if they did in any event return home, they must work for the cause of peace.

50

Amin's use of the word 'if' sent a shiver down the spines of the Israelis.

He then expressed concern for their welfare and asked what they required. 'Mattresses and blankets', they replied. He promised their request would be fulfilled and that even the hostages found that, at least on this point, Idi was true to his word – they were given new mattresses from which the nylon covers had still not been removed, clean blankets and even towels.

The mounting tension of the squad of terrorists, because Israel had not yet succumbed, was becoming noticeable. Most of the Israeli hostages hoped in their heart that their government would relax its consistent policy not to free imprisoned terrorists, although the implication of such a waiver was clear to them. Some did not even conceal their view that Israel must not hand over terrorists. In the conversations among themselves during the long, sweltering hours in the detention hall the die-hard Israelis declared: 'It would be wrong to return them. If we give in this time, who knows what they'll demand tomorrow?'

Others asserted expressly and out of a deep inner conviction, 'If it is our lot to become the sacrifice, then so be it, but not just to return the dozens of terrorists'.

All kinds of plans buzzed around in the minds of some of the captives. But what was there to be done in such conditions? To overpower Idi Amin and use him as a hostage, someone suggested. His listeners burst out laughing. The Ugandans, they said, would be glad to get rid of him. Eitan Aharonowitz and seven other captives decided 'not to go like lambs to the slaughter'. If all hope vanished, they would overcome their guards with bottles, their teeth and their nails.

None of them entertained the fantastic notion that the long arm of the Defence Army of Israel would stretch out so far as Entebbe. . .

Sarah Davidson in her diary:

'All these years I didn't comprehend what the Holocaust meant. Year after year I read over-and-over again what is published on this subject and I see the films and I listen again to the dreadful testimonies. And I don't understand. Why did the Jews file quietly and abjectly into the gas-chambers? Why did they go like sheep led to the slaughter, when they already had nothing left to lose?

I needed this nightmare at Entebbe to help me understand. Now, only now, I understand. It's easy to deceive people who so much want to live. They, the Jews in the Holocaust, did not know what fate awaited them and believed the lies about labour camps and showers. It was easy to fool them.

The German woman was an evil beast. Frustrated as a human being and also as a woman. But at least she was the least dangerous because she did not hide her feelings and did not wear a mask. I would never dream of talking to her. She was the known enemy.

But, in contrast, the male German behaved pleasantly. He was the secret enemy, pretending, luring his victims into trusting his good intentions. He was so quiet, so pleasant, so indulgent – that after the conversations with him I caught myself as being self-accused. You believed him! He succeeded in fooling you! Had he told me to march in a particular direction, where his comrades would be waiting for us there with machine-guns, ready to mow us down – we would have gone. Because he knew how to smile and pretend. He lost no opportunity to tell us. You're not to blame. You're all right. Nothing will befall you. Don't worry. Your government will agree to the swap and you'll be flown home. And because we wanted so much to believe that he was different from the others, better than the others, more amenable than the others – we believed him. But no one had to push this "good German" into emptying all the magazines full of bullets at our children, to blow us up with grenades or to set off the booby-trap explosives.'

Idi Amin, who at the outset of the episode wanted to pose to the world as the 'saviour' of the captives, liberated forty-seven of those detained, all of non-Israel nationality, and especially women, children, elderly persons and the sick. They reached Orly airport outside Paris on Wednesday, 30 June. The world learned from their lips for the first time the full particulars of the conditions which the hostages in Uganda were suffering, and the separation between the Israelis and the other passengers.

Their liberation, they said, had been secured as a result of negotiations which Idi Amin conducted with the hijackers. And who could have told them that except Idi Amin himself . . .

The families of the captives back in Israel were gnawed by grave anxiety. Their fears mounted daily and reached the peak on the day the Israeli press announced on their front pages the 'selection', Uganda-style.

The mother of one of the captives described how she felt in those days of dread: 'My son had planned this trip to Europe a long time and saved up for it penny-by-penny. We were none too keen about his going on it, but when we saw how much he wanted it, we hadn't the heart to stop him. So off he went'.

From the first day that they heard over the radio that the aircraft had been hijacked, she went on, they did not sleep a wink. Their lives went on between one newscast to the next. They bought up all the newspapers. Maybe one of them would have a detail that was not in the others. They read and went mad. The hijackers threatened dire punishment.

When the plane was making its way southwards from Athens, they were afraid it would be blown up in the air. Maybe they'd open fire inside the plane and someone would be hit . . . And when it came down in Libya, they were even more afraid. How to get out of there? They rushed round to the Air France offices, she said, to find out whether maybe it was not the plane after all, maybe it had landed at Athens? But no. It was the plane.

Then the telephones began to ring. Everyone somehow knew that their son was in this plight. They didn't know what to say. The radio was switched on all the time. Every scrap of news sent them jangling to their feet, frightening them. They listened to all the silly songs that were being played in order not to turn off the set and miss a piece of news. Perhaps someone would say what had happened to their child.

'The very name "Libya" alone scared us. Who knew what that Ghaddafy would do to them?' she went on. 'Several madmen inside, one madman outside, and our child trapped in all this business. . .

When the plane took off from Libya we began to be afraid again, in case it was blown up in the air. Where to now? Maybe they'd be taken to Israel? And if here, maybe they'd blow it up here? Lunacy, lunacy, but what was he doing in that plane? Was he all right? Had those beasts harmed him? . . .'

The hours crept by, every one an eternity. They switched from one station to another on the set. Perhaps one of them had something new, that the other had not broadcast. No, it was all the same. The plane was in Uganda. Then it was announced that the passengers had got off the plane. 'We thought that the terrorists were conducting some "exercises" or something like that and would kill everyone, but it didn't happen.

'We didn't even know where Uganda was. We took a map and searched for it, and when we found the place, we knew that somewhere, in some tiny spot, there was our son. And why all this? Had we not suffered enough in the past, that he should now have to suffer too?

Then later we learned what they demanded. Murderers in exchange for our boy. Fear continued to grip us with its full force. Would their demands be accepted? That is to say, would we see him again, here, in this room? Or, perhaps, the people wouldn't be let go and then ... We knew it was a principle and that Israel served the world as an example of no surrender to terrorists, but all this was being said about our child. And we wanted our child back alive and not principles ...

'Until the moment the hijackers announced their ultimatum, all that had happened until then seemed to be nothing to what it was now', she continued. 'It was like a death warrant. So many more hours, so many more minutes – would the most dreadful thing of all be done to them? Would they harm my child, somewhere there in the passenger hall at the end of the world?

We tried to imagine the place, to imagine where he sat. We saw him veritably with our eyes. I shall always remember those hours all my life. My heart was breaking. A helpless child. Someone could save him, but nothing was being done.'

Meanwhile the Committee of Relatives launched energetic action. 'No, no, I didn't go to the meetings. Why? I don't know. I had already read in the afternoon papers about the "selection" that had been carried out there. I trembled. I thought that this term, "selection", had disappeared from the world of the Jewish people, and here it had come back. I read how the rescued French people, who were released because they were not Israelis, told of the horrible things they had undergone. I wondered if our son too would be privileged to tell us the story? When would he be freed?'

The representatives of the families of the captives in Uganda met the French Ambassador in Israel, Jean Herly, and proposed to him that M. Jacques Chiraq, the French Prime Minister, should fly to Entebbe and remain there until the release of the hostages – this as a tangible indication that France was determined to fulfill its promises.

The Government of Israel identified itself with the feelings of the families and understood their motivations in making the demands they did; but it was out of the question that its considerations should be outweighed by the emotions of people whose dear ones were held by terrorists, nor even by public opinion in Israel or the world at large. The Government must act in accordance with one and only one criterion – the supreme, long-range interest of the State of Israel.

It was according to these lights that the Rabin government, as past governments in Israel, determined the principles of its policy – as long as an alternative existed, there could be no surrender to terrorist blackmail. The words 'as long as there is an alternative', were as sharp as a double-edged sword.

Israel had diverged from this policy on two solitary occasions previously, when it had no other option. It was when Israeli civilian aircraft had been hijacked and landed in hostile countries, and Israel paid the price, the release of terrorists, in return for the freeing of an El Al plane taken to Algeria and the liberation of two Israelis removed from a T.W.A. airliner and incarcerated in Damascus.

The snatch of the El Al plane and its forced landing in Algeria was the first time this had ever happened to an Israeli aircraft and the government policy was formulated and consistently pursued as a consequence of that incident.

It would now seem that the Government had been confronted by one of those no-other-option situations. The Prime Minister and his associates in the government were fully aware that submission to the terrorists would endow international terror with a decisive victory and create a dangerous precedent. Because this time a sovereign state was co-operating with the air-pirates.

This latter fact had now been proved beyond all doubt in the light of the reports brought back by the first batch of liberated passengers. Fulfilment of the will of the hijackers would engender most serious implications and be a dangerous erosion of anti-terror actions.

Nor was that the only exceptional aspect of the hijacking. There were other aspects: the gunmen had made it a condition that criminals serving jail terms in other countries be included in any bargain for freeing the hostages. If Israel were to ask these other governments to respond to the demand and release terrorists in their prisons in order to save the lives of Israeli citizens, it was clear that a similar gesture would have to be made in future and criminals imprisoned in Israel be allowed to go scot free every time a plane was snatched – or a train or any foreign nationals kidnapped in whatever country for purposes of blackmail.

The Israeli government was bound not to allow the situation to deteriorate in this manner. On the other hand, would this refusal serve as the green light for the Entebbe gunmen to massacre dozens of Israeli citizens in cold blood? The circle was closed: it appeared that, in spite of everything, no other option than to give in was available.

Certainly, the military option had been assessed daily, in the light of the changing data and information, from the first reports of the hijacking, but no way to give it palpable form had been worked out.

Meanwhile the deadline fixed by the terrorists was approaching and the exchanges with Idi Amin, who had agreed to mediate through the medium of the French Government for 'humanitarian reasons', only strengthened the fear that the gunmen would in fact carry out their threats.

When it transpired on the Monday that Idi Amin was actually collaborating in the hijacking aftermath, the Prime Minister decided to associate the leaders of the parliamentary opposition in all the processes of decisions.

Before he reported on the situation to the Foreign and Security Affairs Committee of the Knesset, the Prime Minister met with Knesset members Menahem Begin and Elimelech Rimalt, Opposition chiefs, and brought them up-to-date on current developments. Begin declared that the Prime Minister could rely in this hour on the full support of the parliamentary opposition.

Early in the morning of Thursday, 1 July, the Prime Minister convened in his office the special team of ministers that had been set up to deal with the affair. The purpose of the deliberations this time was, as he stated, 'to crystallize thinking' in advance of the discussion scheduled to be held at a special Cabinet session later that morning.

Time went on inexorably. The ultimatum pronounced at Entebbe was due to expire in a few hours, at midday. Idi Amin had announced that the terrorists had booby-trapped the terminal and were preparing to give effect to their threat to blow up the structure with its hostages unless their demands were complied with.

The relatives of the hostages, with whom the Israel authorities were in close touch and from whom nothing was hidden, were seized by understandable panic and exerted pressure on the ministers to accede to the gunmen's fiat. At that time there were no differences of outlook among the ministers and complete unanimity of views existed as to the need to proclaim the readiness of the Government of Israel to enter into negotiations with the hijackers. The Foreign and Security Affairs Committee and opposition leaders were of the same opinion.

At 8.30 in the morning the Government announced it was ready to negotiate with the terrorists. The ultimatum weighed down as a heavy shadow. It was not clear exactly when it would expire. Lieutenant-Colonel (Reserves) Baruch Bar-Lev, regarded as the closest friend of the ruler of

Uganda, was asked by the Government to contact Idi Amin in order to find out the precise deadline.

Baruch ('Burka') Bar-Lev, a highly experienced Israeli army officer, had spent five years in Uganda as the head of the Defence Ministry mission during the period in which Israel extended generous aid to Uganda and even supervised the training of its army. Personal ties had developed between Baruch Bar-Lev and Idi Amin even before the latter had become President of his country and served as the Chief of Staff of the Ugandan Army.

When Bar-Lev arrived in Uganda, Idi Amin was still a 'green' novice as Chief of Staff. He had previously served in subordinate grades in the British Army and this epoch had imprinted resentment and sombre memories on his mind. To refrain from reviving the memories of those times, Bar-Lev was careful not to wear uniform when meeting Amin, and when the latter began to suffer aches and pains in the joints of his arms and feet, Burka suggested that he visit Israel and bathe in the waters of the Dead Sea or the sulphur baths at Tiberias.

Amin accepted the invitation and during his stay in Israel was examined by a specialist in the disease which he had contracted. The latter was of the opinion that the malady could not be cured but it was possible to slow down its course by diet and the use of medicines.

To ensure that Idi Amin would not forget to take the medicaments regularly, they were given to his close associates – his driver, his secretary and a member of his family – to administer to him. Idi Amin was grateful to Burka for having organized his visit to Israel.

At that time the President of Uganda, Milton Obote, had been displaying a hostile attitude to Israel and in 1971 even intended to expel the Israelis from his country. Idi Amin, then his Chief of Staff, blocked this intention by reason of his justified pro-Israeli views which had been formed to a large extent by his close ties with Bar-Lev.

One day when a Ugandan brigadier-general named Okea, a member of the Acholi tribe, had been murdered, President Obote planned to exploit the assassination to oust Amin, and he started the rumour that the Chief of Staff had been involved in it.

Idi Amin was then in Cairo at the invitation of the Egyptian Minister of Defence. President Obote summoned him back urgently to Kampala. Sensing that something was wrong, Amin contacted Bar-Lev through an intermediary and asked him to find out what was happening.

Bar-Lev was placed in an awkward position. He feared any involvement, but at the same time he knew that the deposing of Amin meant an end to the friendship between Uganda and Israel and the expulsion of the latter from its important key-position on the African continent.

Bar-Lev communicated with Amin's fellow-tribesman, the Ugandan Minister of Defence, Felix Onema, and consulted him. Onema investigated the matter and learned that Obote was planning to detain Amin on his return to Uganda on the trumped-up charge of having assassinated the brigadier-general.

'It's a pretext', Bar-Lev declared, adding, 'You've done a great thing in coming to me. A great thing for Uganda. I'll go to the airport myself to receive Idi and escort him to Parliament House'.

In this way Idi Amin was saved from imprisonment through the initiative and help of the Israeli officer and their friendship was cemented. It was Bar-Lev who counselled Amin to form an élite unit in his army of the size of a battalion to consist of two paratroop companies, a squadron of tanks and a squadron of recoilless gun-carrying jeeps, made up of men ready to protect him at any time, should President Obote make a move to kill him.

That, in effect, was the origin of the idea to establish paratroop and armoured forces in Uganda. Amin's imagination was fired by it and Israeli paratroop and armour instructors were posted to the country to train Ugandans in those crafts.

It soon came about that his special troops were called upon to save Idi Amin. A further attempt to oust him was launched by Obote in 1971 when he was away with his entourage at Singapore, attending a British Commonwealth conference. The officer commanding an army battalion stationed in Kampala was ordered to undertake the arrest of Amin. The battalion commander fell in with the scheme and secretly convened together several officers loyal to him at a meeting at the Officers' Club. The coup was meant to put an end to the careers of Idi Amin and his adherents.

Four Ugandan parachute instructors who were loyal to Amin happened to be in the place and, on learning the reason for the meeting, they killed all those present. After the event Amin telephoned Bar-Lev and told him, 'The revolution has started'.

Bar-Lev's wife, Nehama, and their four children were also on good terms with Idi's wives and children. Each family often visited the other.

The Israeli officer came to have an intimate knowledge of what motivated Idi Amin, especially after he had taken over the reins of power, and found, to his shock, that here was an unbalanced man who was totally unreliable.

Bar-Lev first revealed his opinion of Amin to his associates at a conference held in 1970 in Israel of Defence Ministry mission chiefs from all parts of the world. The Defence Minister's then special assistant, Lieutenant-General (Reserve) Zvi Tzur, who was astounded by the revelations, exclaimed, 'You're exaggerating!' Bar-Lev replied, 'On the contrary, the truth is much more acute'.

It was with all these circumstances in mind that Bar-Lev,

responding to the request of the Government of Israel, picked up the telephone in his villa in a pleasant countryside suburb north of Tel Aviv, dialled Idi Amin's number in Kampala and waited for an answer.

Bar-Lev had spoken to the Ugandan ruler before this. The following telephone conversation, every word of which he had tape-recorded, was a long one which had begun at two o'clock the previous afternoon. It went as follows:

BAR-LEV: The President?

AMIN: Who's that speaking?

BAR-LEV: Colonel Bar-Lev.

AMIN: How are you, my friend?

BAR-LEV: How do you feel, sir?

AMIN: I'm very glad to hear your voice today.

BAR-LEV: I'm speaking from my home. I've heard what has happened, my friend. May I ask you to do something?

AMIN: I agree, because you're my good friend.

BAR-LEV: ... My friend, you have a great opportunity to go down in history as a great peacemaker. As there are many people in England, the United States and in Europe who write bad things about you, you have a chance to show them that you're a great peacemaker, and if you release the people you'll go down in history as a very big man. I thought about all this this morning, when I heard all these things on the wireless.

AMIN: ... I successfully spoke with the 'Popular Front' of Palestine. They released forty-seven hostage passengers. They have of course in their possession a total of 145 Israelis and Jews together, and other hostages. Altogether 250 ... I have just released forty-seven hostages and handed them over to the French Ambassador. It's very important for you to listen to Radio Uganda at five o'clock this afternoon.

BAR-LEV: What about the Israeli hostages?

AMIN: The 'Popular Front' of Palestine are now surrounding the remaining hostages completely – they say that if the Israeli Government doesn't answer the demand, they will blow up the French plane and all the passengers at twelve noon (Greenwich Mean Time) tomorrow. Therefore I propose to you, my friend, to report to Rabin – General Rabin, the Prime Minister, I know him – he is my friend, and to General Dayan, I know he is my friend although he isn't in the government, and your government must do everything possible to release these hostages immediately, that is the demand of the Palestinians. I am doing the best I can and give them mattresses, blankets, food, medical attention and there's someone getting medical assistance in hospital and at the doctor's advice will be flown to Paris, when the doctor approves this. I want you to do everything possible. I spoke with all the Israelis now and they're very glad. And so their words are recorded on television. They asked me to send this notice to the government . . . immediately.

BAR-LEV: Mr President, you are the governor of this country. I think you have the power to release these people. You'll go into history as a great man.

AMIN: I want you to know that you are my friend for always . . . I told the American journalists that Colonel Bar-Lev is my friend. I shall be very glad to see you, because I know you well. I am ready to make peace between Israel and the Arabs. And I want you to tell this seriously to your government, anything you want of me – let me know. Report to your government to send a statement through the French, that I want to save the lives of the Israelis by their accepting the demands of the Palestinians.

BAR-LEV: Can you do something to stop them from killing?

AMIN: I can stop them, if your government accepts their demand immediately . . . now they're calling me. Their final decision will be published at five. And so it is necessary to act before tomorrow at twelve o'clock. Otherwise they will blow up the plane and kill all the hostages. Your government must do everything possible.

BAR-LEV: Mr President, do you remember your mother, who told you before she died, that you should help the Israelis from the Holy Land. If you want to be a great and holy man and go into history, and even perhaps receive the Nobel Prize, then save these people ... It's a grand opportunity. It has been given you by God, to show everyone that you're a great and good man.

AMIN: How are you, my friend? How is your wife?

BAR-LEV: Everything is all right. Would you like me to come to you?

AMIN: I shall be glad to see you.

BAR-LEV: Can you stop them from killing until I come to you?

AMIN: Can you go to your government tomorrow, so that I can have an answer?

BAR-LEV: Very well, my friend. I shall talk to you again later.

AMIN: Telephone me whenever you like. I am waiting ... I am speaking from the airfield. I have not slept for three days. I want to save the lives of these people.

At 11.05 that same night a further telephone conversation was held between 'Big Daddy' and Bar-Lev:

BAR-LEV: I have transmitted your advice through my friend to the government ... He told me that they received your suggestion and will act in this matter through the Government of France, as you suggested ... Now I am trying to find a way of coming to visit you ...

AMIN: If you come here, you will feel like at home ... because you are my good friend. No one will harm you.

BAR-LEV: I can trust in you and in God, not in anyone else.

AMIN: My daughter, Sharon, sends you regards.

BAR-LEV: Thank you, Your Excellency. Until I have an opportunity to come and visit you, will you take all the necessary measures and make sure that nothing will happen to the hostages?

AMIN: I am now with the leader of the Palestinian 'Popular Front'. He has just come. He is the man who decides ... The man with whom I negotiated previously was their number two in the command. Now the proper man has arrived. He told me about forty minutes ago that he would not change the decision if he did not receive any reply until ten o'clock Uganda time tomorrow morning ...

BAR-LEV: Your Excellency, I am doing my very best to come and see you. I may be of benefit to you ... When I heard the news on the wireless I said "Now Idi Amin Dada my friend has got his good opportunity, his biggest chance to do something very big." Everyone will speak about you. Please, stop all the bloodshed. I will try to come to you and find another solution.

AMIN: But they have now moved the 145 Jews together and they say they will surround them with explosives, and so an answer must be given at once.

BAR-LEV: I am a private person ... If you remember, I always gave you good advice and never once gave you bad advice. Right? ... This is your country and you are the President and you have the power. If something happens, you will be blamed; and if you save the people, you will be a holy man. What is the situation, Your Excellency?

AMIN: They refused. They surrounded everyone and they say they can blow up all the hostages and all the Ugandan Army who are around them ...

BAR-LEV: Yes, I understand. I don't think they have so much explosives. How can they come in a plane with such a large quantity of explosives? ... Your Excellency, I want you to understand that they are asking the release of murderers who committed many murders. They killed women and children. I don't believe that even you, if someone tried to kill you, would let him go. It's not easy to persuade people here to release murderers. You must understand that I am speaking because I know you as a soldier. You will never give in and release a murderer, so that it isn't easy to do a thing like this. I am sure that you, as President of the State, will not let anyone decide what to do in your country.

AMIN: I agree with what you say completely. But the position is now very complicated, because these people have even brought on their bodies a full load of T.N.T. (trinitrotoluene) – and that is very complicated.

BAR-LEV: Sir, it will take me a day or two until I can come to you and help you ... can you keep them quiet for at least two days?

AMIN: But they refused and said that the last time is tomorrow at ten o'clock to noon. They won't wait for me, they said they will all commit suicide with all the hostages. They've already prepared everything to press (the button), so as to explode together with themselves.

BAR-LEV: Where are the people – in a hotel or the plane? Where do they sleep?

AMIN: They are in the old airfield at Entebbe ... We have built a modern airport ... The old field has only a building and that's where they are holding all the hostages ... There's no plane there. They asked that all the planes be removed. All of the Air Force are now outside Entebbe. They've put the explosives around everything ... Two rows of explosives inside and outside. They came with explosives in the plane, in boxes. I think that certain people, perhaps in Athens, agreed not to examine the boxes ...

BAR-LEV: Where is the French plane?

AMIN: Near to me. They have a number of people inside it with explosives ... They are ready to explode it ... You can help me if you tell your government to release these persons, those whom you call criminals ... It's better to save the lives of more than 200 people ... They said they're going to kill completely. They'll begin with blowing up the plane, and then they'll kill everyone at once with explosives. They said that if any plane comes over Uganda – they'll blow up everything immediately ...'

While the details of the conversations of the day before were still fresh in his mind, he heard Idi Amin's voice once again. This time there were no unnecessary introductions. At the outset of the conversation Idi Amin repeated to Bar-Lev that the announcement of the 'Front for the Liberation of Palestine' would be broadcast at eleven o'clock and that the Government of Israel must listen to it.

BAR-LEV: Sir, how did it happen that more 'Front' men arrived in Uganda? There were only six on the plane, and now there are more than six ... twenty or more ... how did they come in?

AMIN: They were in the plane. There weren't only four, there were thirty from all parts of the world. No one came into Uganda on another plane. For your information, I tried to put all the captives on buses and drive the buses in another direction, but the hijackers wanted that they should be brought to the old airport. This is very difficult for me, I have done the best I can, I think that your government is responsible for the fate of all the Israelis and all the passengers who have double nationality and all the other captured people ...

BAR-LEV: Don't be influenced by the people of the National Front because they are sitting at your side and telling you all kinds of stories ...

AMIN: I am not influenced by the Liberation Movement. I

make my own decisions ... You must also consider my position. You must not insult me, as you have just done, that you say I am collaborating with the kidnappers who are not clean people ...

BAR-LEV: I know three things about you – that you are a great soldier, a great Ugandan and a man who trusts in God. In this case I think you can prevent a slaughter and bloodshed. No one can give you orders. You do what is good for the people of your country and at the command of God. People from outside have no right to do things on the soil of your country.

AMIN: They surrounded the hostages with explosives and they pushed away my soldiers and the lives of the hostages are in their hands ...

BAR-LEV: You can tell them that they are your guests and that they are putting your country in a difficult position ... The people of the 'Front' have never succeeded in doing in Israel what they wanted, although they also had explosives then, because they were not allowed to do this. The world will never accept the argument that you and your great army could not overcome six or ten people ...

AMIN: I know that you say that they were never successful in your country and that I can kill these persons.

BAR-LEV: You are giving them shelter. They stay in Uganda like in a hotel. You are a good friend of the Palestinians and the Arabs. Therefore, they must not put you in a difficult position and cause harm to you. They must not say and think they are operating in Uganda and they don't care what happens in Uganda. They must also consider your problems, and not only you must consider them. You are a good friend of theirs and they must think also of you. Therefore, I think they will not do anything, if Field-Marshal General Idi Amin asks them to do nothing and puts off everything for one day, until I am able to come to you ...

AMIN: I want to tell you that they are not living in a hotel like guests. They are together with the captives and if we do any act we shall endanger the lives of the captives. They also eat together. They are not my guests. I agree that I am a good friend of theirs. I want peace in Palestine. How can we bring peace? That is the responsibility of your government. You must not continue with Zionist activity and with this policy. You must do everything in order to bring peace to Palestine.

Baruch Bar-Lev's efforts in his conversation with Idi Amin to find out the exact time when the ultimatum given by the terrorists would lapse were of no avail. Idi Amin refused to discuss the matter. He suggested that Bar-Lev should get in touch with him once more after the announcement of the 'Front' at eleven o'clock. Bar-Lev reported his conversation to the Government of Israel.

5 Decisions

It was the explicit threat of the Thursday dead-line ultimatum which motivated the Government of Israel to express their readiness to release the imprisoned terrorists. There was a strong feeling that unless something was done, the lives of the hostages would be imperilled. The most important result achieved by the Government of Israel's decision was that the hijackers extended the dead-line until Sunday.

Itzhak Rabin held firm to his opinion that the Government had no moral justification to jeopardize the lives of the captives for the sake of a principle, no matter how important. 'We could not let ninety Israeli citizens be butchered by thugs', he said, 'just because of a principle not to exchange them under specific conditions.'

Entebbe: Thursday, 1 July. Time was running out like the sand in an hour-glass. Forty minutes remained until the expiry of the ultimatum at two o'clock that afternoon. The fortunes of the hostages would be determined for good or ill unless, in that span of trickling sand, forty terrorists, serving jail terms in Israel, and sixteen in other countries, were released (or at least consent to release them was expressed). The alternative was a blood-bath.

Suspense mounted, nerves were stretched taut. The captives themselves were aware of the situation. It was no secret to them that Israel had not surrendered even once in the preceding seven years to terrorist blackmail of this kind. Each one of them tried not to think about the ordeal ahead,

1 General Benjamin Peled, Commander of the Israeli Air Force

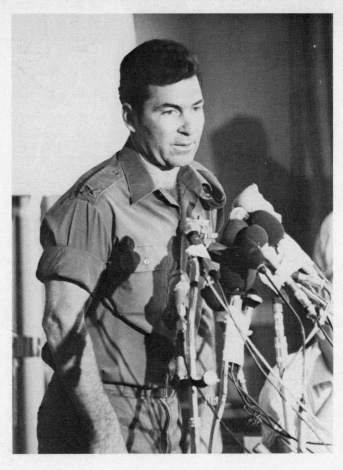

2   General Dan Shomron, Commander of the action at Entebbe

3   The Commander of the Israeli strike force at Entebbe, Lieutenant-Colonel Jonathan 'Yoni' Netanyahu, who was killed during the action

4   Soldiers pouring out of a 'Hercules' plane

5 Mordechi Gur, Chief of Staff, and Shimon Peres, Minister of Defence, at the press conference after the action

6 The pilot of the hijacked Air France jet coming out of the 'Hercules'

7 & 8 The returned hostages being welcomed by their relatives

but it was more than the human spirit could endure, and the anxiety could barely be repressed.

The clock ticked on inexorably, minute by minute. Suddenly, the captives witnessed the spectacle of a staid, middle-aged man running with all the strength he could muster towards the doorway to the terminal building. It was the French Ambassador to Uganda, Pierre Renard.

'Israel is ready to negotiate', the Ambassador gasped, his excitement evident through his laboured breathing.

The same excitement gripped the captives, their nerves and minds relieved of a heavy load. They burst spontaneously into applause, clapping hands gleefully.

Israel had given in. The unbelievable had happened.

Without further ado, the authorities in Jerusalem sped messages to France and West Germany conveying their decision, with explanations of the considerations which had actuated it. Reaction was mixed. One senior French official expressed a mingled comment. 'We understand your dilemma, but nothing good will come of your decision. Just as many other countries in the world are beginning to get tough with kidnappings, Israel is "folding".'

Ever since the hijackers' demands had been declared from Entebbe those Western European governments which were involved in the affair waited to know Israel's attitude before formulating their own policies. They breathed with relief when Israel announced a readiness to talk.

Feverish consultations were opened immediately between Bonn and Paris. The West German government faced a particularly knotty problem – there were no German nationals aboard the hijacked plane but the captors were demanding the release of six dangerous criminals in return for the freeing of hostages holding other nationalities.

The authorities at The Hague did not respond officially. Among the passengers was only one Dutch family, the wife and children of a diplomat who was posted in Indonesia, and they were among the forty-seven people of non-Israeli nationality who had been released at Entebbe and flown to Paris. But even before this gesture the press in the Netherlands found no special interest in the episode, nor even published an editorial comment about it.

It would appear that public opinion in France showed little surprise at Israel's decision. A commentator on 'Europa 1' explained to listeners in his broadcast that Israel had been compelled to take account of the interests of other countries. Moreover, he stressed this time that military option was denied to Israel because of distance . . .

But no one queried the decision nor opposed it. The governments of Israel and France agreed to set up a joint negotiating team in Paris in which the former would be represented by its Ambassador in France, Mordecai Gazit. Foreign Minister Yigal Allon, telephoned from Jerusalem to his French opposite number, Jean Sauvenargues, and obtained his consent for the exchange of the hostages and terrorists to take place in France, giving as the reason that the plane was French.

On Friday morning the Government of Israel learned that 101 captives had been freed at Entebbe and had reached Paris. Those left in terrorist hands in Uganda were holders of Israeli citizenship, dual nationality – Israel and other countries – and a number of Jews of various nationalities.

The government ministers in Jerusalem received the news with mixed feelings. On the one hand, the fact that only Israelis and Jews remained at Entebbe turned the affair into an exclusive problem for Israel, and increased the fear that the terrorists really intended to carry out their threat to murder the hostages. On the other hand, if it transpired that a military option existed, and at this stage it was no more than speculation, then this at least was better.

Meanwhile, a high-ranking army reserve officer, Major-General Rehoboam Ze'evi, known far and wide in Israel by the nickname 'Ghandi', who was Special Adviser on Intelligence to the Prime Minister, had been staying in Paris and had gathered valuable information from the released passengers. There were still 109 captives at Entebbe.

The negotiations began. They were conducted in the most extraordinary manner through six mediators. The circuitous route went as follows:

Messages from the Prime Minister's Office in Jerusalem went to the Israeli Embassy in Paris by telephone or telex. They were then sent from the Embassy on the Right Bank of the River Seine to the special staff set up for the purpose in the French Foreign Ministry on the Quai d'Orsay, situated on the Left Bank of the Seine. The French Foreign Minister himself officially headed the special staff unit, assisted by the Director-General of the Ministry, M. de la Beaulieu, who was in actual charge of the team-work.

From the French Foreign Ministry the communications from Israel were sent to the French Ambassador at Kampala, Pierre Renard, through the regular international telephone exchange because France had no direct telephone cable or wireless connections with Uganda.

M. Renard transmitted the messages to the Somali Ambassador at Kampala (who, incidentally, was an avowed supporter of the Palestine Liberation Organization), and the latter was in direct touch with –

Idi Amin, the hijackers at Entebbe and Wadie Hadad.

The replies from the hijackers took the same route – in reverse.

The Somali Ambassador declared from the very first that the terrorist group in Uganda were not prepared to enter into any bargaining process with Israel over the number of jailed terrorists to be returned. Every one of them must be freed. In addition, the hijackers regarded Israel as responsible for the release of the others held in Germany, Switzerland and Kenya. In other words, there was nothing to negotiate about. Israel could do nothing but give in and accept their demands.

However, it soon became evident that the hijackers were not satisfied with their own original terms. They now demanded the release of more criminals imprisoned in Israel for other offences.

The negotiations dragged on. Valuable time was being lost in the exchange of messages through roundabout channels. The dead-line was approaching. In spite of the considerable worries and perplexities, Israel was doing its best not to shirk its role in the tortuous interchanges.

Among other questions that posed difficult decisions was the place where the exchange of hostages and released convicts would be carried out. Israel felt apprehensive about the choice of Entebbe, on which the hijackers insisted, because it was possible that they were preparing some sort of trap under the courteous auspices of Idi Amin. They were liable, for instance, to make more demands, after having received the full number of released criminals which they now requested, and before releasing the captives, if at all.

Israel wanted the exchange to take place in France, the country which was responsible from the legal standpoint for the welfare and safety of the captives. It became more and more apparent as the protracted process of negotiations went on, and the hijackers' terms were augmented, that no common decision by the countries involved could be achieved by the time the new ultimatum set by the men at Entebbe expired – eleven o'clock G.M.T. on Sunday morning, 4 July.

The authorities in Jerusalem decided to send to Paris its former Ambassador to France, Asher Ben-Nathan, now political adviser to the Minister of Defence, to find out precisely what the Entebbe terrorists wanted, and to discover if there was any actual possibility of obtaining the liberation of the hostages by negotiation.

It transpired that there was no one in France dealing with the matter who was prepared to promise Ben-Nathan that some sort of arrangement would in fact be reached with the hijackers.

The desperate nature of this news spurred the Minister of Defence, Shimon Peres, and the Minister of Transport, Gad Ya'acobi, into broaching an unusual suggestion – to send the former Defence Minister, Moshe Dayan, as a special emissary to Uganda. Both men hoped that Moshe Dayan would be able to persuade Idi Amin, who professed a cordial friendship for 'General Dayan' whom he had known for a long time, to adopt a more reasonable stand.

Both Itzhak Rabin and his Foreign Minister, Yigal Allon, turned down the proposal. Neither of them trusted Idi Amin's 'friendliness' to Dayan, and the Prime Minister argued that the latter was likely to become an additional hostage in the hands of the hijackers, who would regard him as far more valuable and important than any of the others they held. The idea was dropped altogether when Rabin emphasized that Idi Amin's reactions and whole behaviour were demonstrably 'unpredictable', to use his own words.

Since Idi Amin, the former heavyweight boxing champion and Chief of Staff of the Ugandan armed forces, had seized the reins of power in his country more than five years ago, Uganda had paid an enormous price for that privilege in human lives, estimated at 50,000 persons at least and ranging to as high as 200,000 by some evaluations.

He had recently even appointed himself to be President for life. The powers of the judiciary and of the civilian administration were rescinded and the army was permitted to carry out arrests at its own discretion. His troops rampaged and looted shops without let or hindrance, robbed passers-by in broad daylight and behaved as they wished, with complete impunity, throughout the length and breadth of that unfortunate country.

During the period in which he served as Chief of Staff, Amin blocked the promotion of those officers who were educated and were professionally competent, and advanced cadets and backward elements. By this he sought to create a solid barrier around himself against those who surrounded him, and forestall any chance of effective competition. The same motivation led him to make frequent changes in the command, structuring and composition of his army without heed to any visible or perceptible professional ability.

'Bid Daddy' lived in constant fear of a revolt that would divest him of power by the same method which he had used towards Milton Obote, the previous President. That was the reason for the continual presence around him of soldiers who were loyal to him, who maintained a strict watch, and who were themselves subject to the vigilant supervision disguised under the name of 'Public Investigation Unit'.

By June 1976 there had been eight attempts on Idi Amin's life. The last of them, perpetrated five weeks prior to the hijacking of the French air-bus, had resulted in his driver being killed and thirty-seven persons in his entourage suffering varying degrees of injury. But he himself emerged unscathed, whole and hearty, without a scratch. This lucky escape apparently fortified his faith that 'God is always on my side and not even witchcraft can harm me'.

A perpetual dearth of food developed, the black market flourished and inflation soared. He contributed towards the destruction of the economy by expelling inhabitants of Asian origin, who had made up the majority of the mercantile class, technicians and members of the liberal professions. To keep Uganda afloat on the troubled sea of its storm-tossed economy, he drew closer to the oil-rich Arab countries which granted him financial aid, and established close ties with the

Soviet Union, which began supplying him with considerable armaments, particularly tanks and aircraft.

One reason for the rupture of his good relations with Israel was the latter's refusal to provide his air force with 'Phantom' planes and greater subventions in foreign currency. Prior to this demand, he had asked the Israel Defence Force instructors, who were attached to his service, to set up a navy for him, although Uganda, as is well known, has no sea outlet.

He also complained bitterly that he was not being provided with the armoured columns equipped as he would wish. By his express instructions spectacular 'show' parades (applauded by crowds of onlookers in the fashion of 'organized spontaneity') and military exercises with paratroop drops on target areas were staged. But the paratroops whose parachutes opened after their jumps in these drills were none other than Israeli instructors, as the Ugandan army still had no trained parachutists who could be relied upon for show-case action.

Idi Amin regards himself as successful, more competent and intelligent than other Africans, and with an affinity to Western culture. On the other hand he despises and is opposed to the entire system of the Western way of life.

Nevertheless, he exerts considerable effort to amalgamate with the Occidental body politic, with its ceremonial forms which he says he so greatly loathes. His self-aggrandisement is prominent in almost every step that he takes. Amin feels that he is omnipotent, that he sits at a powerful control centre and directs the affairs of the world by pressing buttons. He is goaded by a compulsion to perform contrary and diametrically opposed acts. His reflexes are unpredictable.

The Israel authorities learned during the course of the negotiations that France had approached the Secretary-General of the United Nations, Dr Kurt Waldheim, to try to secure the liberation of the hostages. The small team of Israeli Ministers had all the time expressed the fear, though keeping it to themselves that France might divest itself of responsibility and transfer it to the United Nations.

Allon spoke with his French counterpart at the Quai d'Orsay. Sauvenargues explained that the approach to the United Nations had been made by France because there had been passengers of different nationalities on board the aircraft. He promised Allon that there was no intention on the part of France to relinquish its responsibility and that President Giscard d'Estaing was behind him in making this promise.

It will be recalled that the hijackers had insisted that the exchange of hostages for freed prisoners should take place on Ugandan soil. But this point was not the only obstacle in the path of the conversations. They brought forward fresh terms from time-to-time, one of which was the payment of five-million dollars in various currencies. It seemed there would be no end to the negotiations while all the time the Sword of Damocles, exemplified by the second ultimatum, was due to fall upon the necks of the hostages at noon on Sunday.

Idi Amin left Kampala on the Friday morning to attend a conference of the Organisation of African Unity in Mauritius. The Government of Israel used the slow-down in the negotiations to continue its consultations in other forums. The Knesset Foreign Affairs and Security Committee heard a report by Amos Eran, Director-General of the Prime Minister's Office, on the latest developments in the indirect contacts with the hijackers.

But Eran was unable to inform the committee of the latest element in the situation – the possibility that began to assume skin and arteries on its naked limbs and that was designed to transform the decision of the Government of Israel from one extreme to the other.

6 The Plan

During the early part of Sunday night following the hijacking of the French air-bus over the Mediterranean, the Chief of Staff and Minister of Defence met and listened to a current report on the air route of the captured aircraft.

Military operational planning started the moment the plane landed on Ugandan soil. The Defence Minister, in full co-ordination with the Prime Minister, began to examine the feasibility of a military option on the morning of Monday, 28 June. The following day the pace of activity in the security sphere speeded up. By noon, while on his way for discussions in Jerusalem, the Chief of Staff, Lieutenant-General Mordecai Gur, gave instructions to set up a planning team for that evening.

The Chief of Staff was asked in the afternoon whether a military option was on the cards, and he answered in the affirmative. From that moment the General Staff went into high gear in planning the operation. The planning teams worked simultaneously on a number of possible lines. The work was done at General Headquarters mainly for reasons of secrecy.

Unlike the situation that prevails in other countries, the government had no need to bring pressure to bear on the army to prepare for the aerial sortie. On the contrary, the army commanders were convinced that it was possible to carry out the rescue operation and all they wanted was to be given the green light by the authorities in Jerusalem. Israel's security had for years been primarily founded on the existence of a highly-trained cadre that could be swung into immediate action with good prospects of success. There is no lack of examples to prove the top-level proficiency of this force. The Defence Army of Israel has carried out many such coups which are remarkable for their daring and audacity.

One of them took place in October 1968 in the period subsequent to the Six-Day War. A commando party led by Colonel Danny Matt flew in a Super-Frelon helicopter to the transformer station at Nedja Hamadi, 450 km south of Cairo. The helicopter landed a short distance away from the station where the raiders spilled out. While the Egyptian soldiers guarding the installations were engaged, sappers laid explosive charges under nine immense oil-containers, the capacity of each of which was about fifty tons, and blew them up in a volcanic eruption of flames and smoke. All were utterly destroyed. As an outcome of this strike, the Egyptian army was compelled to scatter its forces over a wide area to safeguard hundreds of strategic targets in the hinterland of the country.

Another example took place on 28 December 1968. Acting in reprisal for a terrorist attack on an El Al aircraft at the international airport in Athens, the Israel Defence Force carried out a raid on the airport at Beirut and blew up airliners belonging to Arab airlines. The raiders, fully armed, clad in Israeli uniform and wearing red paratroop berets, reached Beirut in four heavy helicopters. With commendable coolness, under the command of Colonel Raphael ('Raful') Eytan, they carried out their mission with clockwork precision.

By the express order of the then Chief of Staff, Lieutenant-General Haim Bar-Lev, they scrupulously avoided harming civilians. They split into two combat units. One went from plane to plane and, after making certain that each belonged to an Arab airline, they primed them with explosives. Simultaneously, the companion unit operated out of sight of the throngs of curious onlookers who were clustering to watch the unusual spectacle and were unaware that this was a military action by a hostile invader. Upon the conclusion of the operation, that lasted only thirty minutes, thirteen aircraft lay smouldering in heaps of metal on the ground and other installations were hit. None of the invaders was hurt. The damage caused was estimated at over a hundred-million dollars.

One of the most renowned exploits carried out by the Israel Army was that which took place during the night of 8–9 September 1969. An armoured force, comprising Russian tanks taken as war booty and anti-armour gun-carriers camouflaged in the colours of the Egyptian army, crossed the Suez Canal in landing-craft and began moving south in Egyptian territory, wiping out Egyptian troops along an axis that went as far as Ras Zafrana, some 90 km south of the city of Suez. Israeli air and naval forces gave support to the land units in close co-ordination.

During the ground action Egyptian surface-to-air missile batteries were hit and damaged, and the entire operation excelled in the fact that the Israeli invaders spent a long time on the west bank of the Suez Canal. A Russian officer, of general's rank, one of the military advisers to the Egyptian army at the time, lost his life when travelling in a car which was crushed in the path of the advancing Israeli column.

Apart from the considerable damage sustained by Egyptian material and installations, the psychological impact of the operation had grave and significant shock-results. A short while after the incursion the Egyptian President, Colonel Gamal Abdul Nasser, suffered a heart attack. Another result was the dismissal of the Chief of the General Staff, General Ahmed Ismail, and other senior ranking officers. The operation was part of the war of attrition which Nasser had foisted upon Israel as an outcome of the 1967 Six-Day War.

Towards the end of 1969 the General Staff of the Israel armed forces resolved to put an end to the operations of the Radar station located in an out-of-the-way spot at Ras 'Arab in the Bay of Suez. The Radar installation, manufactured in the U.S.S.R., was a serious nuisance and obstacle to Israel Air Force aircraft in that area. It was decided that, instead of blowing up the station, it was possible simply to dismantle it and air-lift all the equipment to Israel.

The men of the invading force trained for two days on the dismantling of a Soviet Radar van which had fallen into Israel possession in the Six-Day War. An outstanding Radar technician, serving in the Israel Air Force, was added to the force with the intention of ensuring that the installation would be dismantled without damage to essential parts.

The invaders reached a point twenty-five yards from the Radar station without being detected, and then charged it. Two Egyptian soldiers were killed and four taken captive. The Israeli party disassembled the heavy instruments, roped them up on the hoist-slings of the two helicopters which then took off, and crossed the lines to reach Israel territory safely.

The striking force returned to its base with the four prisoners. The model F-12 Soviet Radar outfit became a centre of interest for intelligence services of the Western world, but it was the Israel Air Force which extracted the maximum advantage from the examination and investigation of its properties.

A direct and powerful 'hit' at an Arab terror organization was carried out by the Israel armed forces on 4 April 1973 when they blew up the Beirut headquarters of the murderous 'Popular Democratic Front' led by Naif Hawatmeh and killed three of its leaders.

The action in the Lebanese capital was planned on the basis of accurate and up-to-date information on the location of the residences of these three men. According to reports originating from and published outside Israel, agents of the intelligence, Mosad, arrived in Beirut the day before the strike and hired swift passenger cars. On the day of the operation these advance men drove in their cars to the beach and waited for the Israeli force which had been landed on the Beirut foreshore from an Israel Navy missile vessel.

Simultaneously, Israeli naval commando units attacked several targets spaced out along the coast of Lebanon in a diversionary operation. During the incursion a large seven-storey building in south Beirut which housed the 'Popular Democratic Front' was blown up and partly demolished, and about forty terrorists were killed in a noisy gun battle. Two of the attacking force fell in the action. The assailants also operated against the 'Fatah' headquarters in the southern section of Beirut. Two workshops engaged in assembling sabotage material, and a garage used by the terrorists north of the port town of Sidon, were razed to the ground.

Without in any way minimizing the difficulties that confronted the planners and executors of the previous commando raids performed by the Defence Army of Israel, nor the flawless and brilliant manner of their performance, the plan for the liberation of the hostages held at Entebbe, though still not finally decided upon, was bound to be radically different. In fact, there was no standard of comparison.

At first glance it seemed that the problems were insoluble – the enormous distance, thousands of kilometres, which the rescue force had to cross in order to reach its target without being discovered by enemy Radar, and the need to land at a strange airfield without arousing the suspicions of the terrorists and the Ugandans, the first reaction of whom would be to slaughter the civilian captives, men, women and children, immured in the terminal building. The bitter experience in the northern Israel village of Ma'alot, where over a score of schoolchildren on an outing had been ruthlessly wiped out, was still fresh in memory.

The planners were working on a number of parallel levels. The aerial problem of transporting the invading force to the arena of action and returning it from there at the conclusion, safeguarding the target zone against Ugandan reinforcements, and medical, logistic and engineering problems.

But the most important of all was planning both a swift eruption into the terminal building and the elimination of the terrorists before they would have time to harm the hostages. Upon this point everyone, from the highest rank down, relied upon one person – Lieutenant-Colonel Jonathan ('Yoni') Netanyahu.

Yoni's reply to the question of whether the operation was practicable constituted the pivot on which all other considerations were built. One Israeli army general even offered the following comment, 'What will it avail us if we overcome the terrorists and the Ugandan army and won't be able to make certain of the rescue of our people?'

Without the need for it to be said, it was clear that Yoni would not only plan the operation in a thousand variations until he reached the best formula, but would also himself command the striking force.

The airfield at Entebbe, which the striking force had to aim at, is on the banks of Lake Victoria. It is an enormous inland sea separated from the runways by a strip of tangled vegetation like that of a botanical garden. The objective of the spearhead force was the old terminal building, a two-storey structure in which the hostages and aircrew of the captured plane were being held. The chief worry was centred on the danger that the terrorists would have time to kill the passengers unless the swoop was swift and the captors could be wiped out swiftly.

This condition dictated the form of the invasion, its planning and the manner of execution: a quick, brief sally that would ensure the liberation of the captives within a few minutes.

Yoni's striking force was very small because of the limitations of the weight of the plane assigned to carry the people. When planning the operation Yoni was confronted by the fact that its success depended upon the rescue force maintaining maximum surprise before the terrorists could react against the hostages. The problem, then, was to land silently and to reach the terminal as quickly as possible.

In commando sallies of this kind the most valuable span of time is between the moment the sentry actually sees what has begun to happen and the moment he realizes what is going on.

Four fundamental considerations were at the heart of the planned action:

First: there had been talk about ten terrorists and from sixty to one hundred Ugandan soldiers in the terminal building – definitely not a negligible force, which had to be attacked with complete surprise.

Second: it would need accurate navigation and pin-point homing-in on the target through the choice of the proper routes and surprise landing. For this purpose it was essential to develop a series of measures that would ensure the initial force arriving at the terminal in as complete a surprise as possible, so that the blow should be sharp, swift and altogether smooth.

Third: a full and meticulous intelligence picture.

Fourth: field security, that is to say, maintenance of secrecy. The order of the Chief of Staff was that no outside factor, no matter how highly placed, must be aware that the operation was in process of preparation.

The risks in various sectors of the enterprise were numerous but these were taken into account during the planning; however awesome, these risks were calculated. The final point which the planners were bound to consider was that the entire action, from the start in Israel until the conclusion in Israel, had to be a wholly Israeli Defence Force operation both in the planning and the execution.

Yoni's men recognized another principle – that swift reaction must be accompanied by maximum caution in order not to harm the hostages. Consequently, the mission was assigned to Yoni and his unit in consideration of their chances of successfully carrying out the raid.

The first plans were shown to the Chief of Staff on Wednesday morning. All of them dwelt on hitting the terrorists but each had its weak points. They could not make sure that the terrorists would not hit back. Also, the accumulated information was still insufficient. It was estimated that one-to-two regiments of Ugandan troops, the number ranging between 500 and 1,000 men, were guarding the airport. It was essential to know where they were posted, how they were doing their guard duty and what weapons they had.

The Chief of the Operations Branch, General Yekutiel Adam, was in charge of the planning. Later on, Brigadier-General Dan Shomron, Chief of the Infantry and Paratroop Corps, was brought into the picture. The commander of the Air Force and his staff unequivocally declared that they could operate in the areas and distance between Israel and Uganda.

Dan Shomron, who was appointed to take charge of the undertaking, went over and over with his officers the possibilities facing the land force. They never lost sight of the fact that the main task was a lightning take-over of the scene of action, a quick dash to the terminal building and annihilation of the hijackers before they were able to molest the captives or, at least, before they could molest many of them.

The aerial aspect, too, came under intensive scrutiny, in the best tradition of a corps that had chalked up innumerable accomplishments, and General Benjamin Peled's reply came sharp and clear. The Air Force was capable of flying the strike force to Uganda in spite of the limitations and bringing it back to Israel.

But the most grave question-mark was still the ground action. The General Staff had stipulated that no plan would be acceptable unless it ensured the immediate extirpation of the terrorists guarding the captives. Yoni laboured unwearyingly to solve this basic problem, but for that purpose he required as full as possible intelligence information.

The intelligence aspect was a chapter in itself in the sphere of planning the action. Exact information was an essential prior condition to the success of so complex an operation. The vast distance from Israel weighed heavily against obtaining the indispensable information.

The Israeli intelligence community searched feverishly for answers to a number of questions: the layout of the airport and what structures were on it; access routes to the terminal building; the points where the Ugandan army were positioned; where the captives were held; where the hijackers were located, and how they watched over their captives; and what was the nature of their firearms.

The intelligence officers closely interrogated the engineers of the great Israeli public works firm, Solel Boneh, which had built the airport at Entebbe on contract during the halcyon period of Israeli-Ugandan relations. But to their mortification the officers learned that the airfield had been enlarged in recent years by an Italian company and consequently there was no advantage to be had from the field plans in the files.

An American news-magazine went as far as to report that the Israeli intelligence approached the Pentagon in Washington D.C. for help, and a West German periodical added that Israel had received satellite photographs of the airport and its environs from the United States.

Vital information, without which there is no doubt that

the operation might not have been feasible, came from the lips of the released passengers who reached Paris.

It was ascertained beyond all doubt that the terminal building was not booby-trapped. Moreover, even if it were to be assumed that the terrorists would run the danger of booby-trapping the hostages under their charge, there can be no question that Idi Amin would not have permitted any such threat to the lives of scores of Ugandan soldiers who, according to the freed passengers, were being held in reserve in the 'rest rooms' on the second floor of the building.

In addition, it was learned that all the captives were quartered in the large hall, but that not all of the sentries were close to them. Several stood guard, whereas their confederates rested in nearby small rooms, or were elsewhere. These facts indubitably helped the planners to lay their scheme of action and it was only after they were obtained that Yoni could complete the plan for the break-through to the terminal, and the Chief of Staff gave his approval and passed it to the government.

General Rehoboam Ze'evi, adviser to the Prime Minister on intelligence, the popularly-known 'Ghandi', was all that time absorbed in gathering essential information for the action, and had been sent to Paris on the Wednesday – three days after the French air-bus was snatched – for the ostensible 'official' purpose of representing the Israel authorities in the contacts with the French over the negotiations proceeding between Paris and Entebbe.

'Ghandi' returned to Israel on Thursday, 1 July, after spending a day in Paris, but went back there when the second party of non-Israeli nationals was released. He was able to collect a good many particulars from them on the projected scene of action.

Tom Ross, columnist on the *Chicago Sun-Times*, claimed that a group of Israeli spies had been at Entebbe before the operation began, first to collect information and then to silence the communications equipment on the field and of the Ugandan army. This was denied by Israeli circles.

Another fascinating story appeared in the German weekly *Der Spiegel* to the effect that the Israelis had apparently sent several combatants to Entebbe in boats. Motor-boats can be hired at Kisumu (in Kenya) without arousing undue attention. Entebbe Airport is situated on the Ugandan side of Lake Victoria. The distance between the shore and the old airport in which the captives were held was only half a kilometre. Only a fence with gaps in it separated the landing runway from the lake.

The German paper went on to claim that, on Friday morning, 2 July, a group of stalwart young men arrived at Wilson Airport, lying about five kilometres from the centre of Nairobi and about ten kilometres from the international airport M'bakasi. They took possession of two, two-motor private planes which they had ordered by telephone the night before. The control tower registered the port town of Kisumu, near Lake Victoria, as the destination of this flight. The next day, on Saturday, both planes were again ordered and flew once more to Kisumu.

The activity of these young reconnaissance pilots from Kisumu is the most credible explanation, in the opinion of *Der Spiegel*, for the perfect arrangements made for the operation on the night of 3 July.

It had been General Adam who tendered the almost complete plan in which every detail was of maximum importance. The Chief of Operations Branch on the General Staff had gone over every stage of the planning in close co-operation with the Air Force commander, General Bennie Peled.

On Thursday evening the Chief of Staff met with the Defence Minister in the latter's home and discussed the plan until the small hours of the night. 'Motta' Gur presented the full plan at first with the words, 'This time I'm presenting the action for "action" '. It was the last of a long series of plans that had seesawed up and down, and of which the common denominator was that they were based on Yoni's judgement and planning. The Chief of Staff's consent, too, was based on Yoni's assurance that the place where the captives were held could be penetrated in a manner that would prevent many casualties.

Actually, the Chief of Staff's affirmative reply to the Government had not been given until he examined each detail minutely. He even joined a 'mock flight' to scrutinize methods of flight and landing in the absence of ground aids. He disembarked from the aircraft only after he was convinced that the flight aspect was 'covered' and that the planes were capable of achieving their mission.

Lieutenant-General Gur made certain on the ground, in a 'model' exercise of a swift break-through to the captives, that the forces scheduled to carry out this part of the operation were fully cognisant of the plan.

It was at that moment that Gur formed his decision to go into action. The quiet self-confidence and responsibility of his commanders served as the binding cement for his professional value-judgement. During his talk with the four pilots and four navigators who had been selected to take part in the flight, he was profoundly impressed by their ability to navigate and improvise, in light of the fact that access to the runway at Entebbe was extremely complicated. The aircrew men gave him their replies soberly and convincingly.

The consultations continued through Saturday morning in the Ministry of Defence offices between Shimon Peres, the Minister, the Chief of General Staff, the heads of the security system and senior army commanders. At that moment the troops were already all prepared to go off on their mission, if it were authorized by the government.

The political decision, reflected thirty-nine-year-old Brigadier-General Dan Shomron at the time, would be much more difficult and daring than the military operation.

As early as Wednesday, 30 June, in conversation with the Minister of Transport, Gad Ya'acobi, Shimon Peres had indicated that the Israel Defence Force was drawing up a plan, but said it was still unready.

The same day, when asked what were the prospects of rescuing the captives, Itzhak Rabin drawled, 'There is a military option and there's a political option, but we still need the data to carry out the military option.'

Ministers were still in unison at the Cabinet meeting on Thursday, 1 July, that at this stage there was no way out other than to negotiate in view of the ultimatum hovering like a storm cloud, and the fear of the hostages being imperilled. Yet at that time the Israel Defence Force had already crystallized a more clear-cut plan, providing an answer to questions which had been unanswerable the day before.

On Thursday evening Gur came to the Defence Minister's home and their discussion of the plan lasted many hours into the night.

On Friday, 2 July, before the final decision was reached by the top political echelon, Peres began to canvas support among these leading elements. He first spoke with the Minister of Justice, Haim Zadok, and won his affirmative reply.

During his 'friendly persuasion' conversations Peres took this line:

'Surrender to the terrorists could be the worst possible thing to happen to the people of Israel at this time. The fact that no free country in the world is pressing us to strike a bargain with the terrorists can be construed as open encouragement to act.'

'It may be', Peres went on to say, 'that there's a risk in the operation and of course there's a risk to the lives of the people there. But the question is – How many other people will be in danger of their lives in future if we succumb to terrorist blackmail?'

Shimon Peres did not hesitate this time, as in the past, to be in close touch with the former Defence Minister, Moshe Dayan, to report to him and get his opinion on the prepared plan, which Peres outlined to him in general terms. Dayan's reply was, 'I'm one hundred and fifty per cent for it.'

It may be supposed that this unambiguous response had a weighty effect, at least in the judgement of the incumbent Minister of Defence.

At nine o'clock on Saturday morning, 3 July, Itzhak called in his associates, Yigal Allon and Peres, for a tripartite discussion with no one else present, neither aides nor members of their staff.

It was on that occasion that Rabin first said 'Yes' to the plan of action. There was no need to persuade Allon; he had from the outset not discounted the military option. Rabin was not oblivious of the fact that an operation of this kind was liable to exact a heavy price and he mentioned the estimated number of casualties, but nonetheless he reached the conclusion that the venture was called for by the urgent dictates of the hour.

One of the issues confronting the Government of Israel before it decided on this foray into Uganda was the encroachment on the sovereignty of that country, and whether this was a breach of the American regulations governing the sale of arms, owing to the utilization of aircraft purchased in the United States. According to these prescriptions, military equipment supplied by the United States could be used only for purposes of internal defence or legitimate self-defence. If any country committed a breach of this regulation, the United States was entitled to demand recovery of the equipment and to cease supplying armaments to the offending country.

On the other hand, in line with the doctrine of self-defence which was anchored in international law, every nation was entitled and even bound to defend its citizens. If it turned out, for instance, that the only way to save the lives of these citizens was by penetrating into another country, then there was legal justification for a direct rescue operation. (It will be recalled that the United States sent its forces into the Congo some years back to rescue missionaries and nuns.)

All nineteen Ministers in the Government of Israel were invited to a conference at two o'clock on Saturday afternoon, in the meeting-hall at the Kirya (government offices) in Tel Aviv, to be informed of the liberation plan and to give their assent.

The Prime Minister sent his driver to the home of the Minister, Zebulun Hammer, an Orthodox Jew, who lived in Bnei Brak, a northern neighbour of Tel Aviv populated mainly by observant Jewish inhabitants, and offered to bring him to the meeting. But the religious Minister preferred to walk from his home to the Kirya in Tel Aviv, and it took him an hour-and-a-half to get there on foot.

Most of the Ministers had not had earlier intimation of the military preparations, and the Prime Minister's announcement was the first intimation that anything was afoot. They were dumbfounded and aghast at the possibility of heavy casualties.

Rabin was insistent upon his view that the action should be proceeded with, 'even if it means losses', and he even gave an estimate – between fifteen and twenty fatalities. Weighing up all the constituent risks, he reached his sombre verdict clear-headedly, and with the assumption in mind

93

that shirking the operation at this juncture would cause untold losses in the future.

During the exchange between the members of the Cabinet, the Interior Minister, Dr Joseph Burg, a devout believer, quoted from the weekly Portion of the Pentateuch in the book of Numbers, *Hukkat* ('the ordinance') and went on to recite these passages:

'And when king Arad the Canaanite, which dwelt in the south, heard tell that Israel came by the way of the spies; then he fought against Israel and took some of them prisoners ...

And the Lord hearkened to the voice of Israel, and delivered up the Canaanites; and they utterly destroyed them and their cities: and he called the name of the place Hormah ...'

Numbers, 21:1, 3

Concluding the quotation, he added, 'Would that we may call Entebbe – *Hormah*!'

The meaning of the Hebrew term *Hormah* is 'utter destruction'.

Consent of the Cabinet to the plan of attack, if secured, was deemed insufficient by the Prime Minister. He called in the Chairman of the Knesset Foreign Affairs and Security Committee, Itzhak Navon, M.K., and the leaders of the Opposition, Knesset Members Menahem Begin and Elimelech Rimalt; and at once before even the Cabinet members had made their decision known, these men heard a full account of the situation given by the Prime Minister and the Chief of General Staff. They supported Rabin's viewpoint and the plan for deliverance of the hostages thereby won the consensus of the Opposition and the Government.

When Rabin told the Opposition leader Begin of his apprehensions concerning a large number of casualties, the latter replied, 'One must always hope for the best. One must believe and try to ensure there'll be no casualties. But if, Heaven forfend, these happen, they'll be of people who fell in battle and not as victims of butchery and savagery'.

Finally it was agreed, 'May the Almighty bless the way of the warriors'.

It may be said that, throughout the successive phases of consultation and consideration, the leadership of the State of Israel rose to a supreme height. Gone were all the dissensions and bickering, large and small, and all collaborated as one body to achieve the objective of safe deliverance of the hostages. The outcome was balanced decisions and wise moves.

It was not easy for Itzhak Rabin to resolve on the execution of the mission. He was fully aware that, should it fail, not only the captive passengers at Entebbe but also the soldiers would pay dearly for the defeat with their lives. He knew no less that it would mean the fall of the Government and the end of his own political career, although it was clear that this point did not enter into his calculations when it came to the question of saving the lives of innocent civilians.

Had the terrorists agreed on Friday, 2 July, to exchange their captives for the jailed gunmen in Israel, without continuing to raise additional demands, it is possible that the Prime Minister might have chosen this course and would not have been compelled to reach the crucial and audacious decision that he did.

Israel did not take counsel with any extraneous factor and no one was asked to help it in this emergency. The Government was swayed by the fact that the terms posed by the terrorists offered no basis for negotiation but were a specific dictate. The resort to military action became more tangible as a possibility on the Friday, but Rabin was finally persuaded of the soundness of the scheme only on Saturday morning.

It has more than once been a matter of speculation and inquiry as to whether the original consent of the Government of Israel to carry out an exchange of hostages for imprisoned terrorists was a ruse in order to win time and dull the vigilance of the hijackers at Entebbe. The answer to this will undoubtedly be found in the personality of Itzhak Rabin. The Prime Minister who is known to be a person of clear incisive thought capable of probing situations with the steel scalpel of his mind, had in all likelihood intended to assure himself of the two options simultaneously: had it become evident that the military option was not feasible, then he would at least have been left with the political option. It was only on the Saturday, when he was convinced that the hostages could be rescued by a military operation, that he decided to choose that alternative.

Rabin's powers of persuasion at the Cabinet session finally bore fruit and the vote was taken at 5.30 p.m. The decision to undertake military action for the deliverance of the people held in custody at Entebbe was adopted unanimously.

While awaiting the government's decision, Dan Shomron, the general officer commanding the paratroops and infantry, who had been chosen to command the ground action, said to one of his units at a military base 'somewhere in Israel': 'The prospect that the government will approve carrying out the plan of action is one-to-nine'.

The commanding officer of the base who was 'hosting' Dan Shomron and his entourage was equally pessimistic and said, 'The only target you'll capture is my office'.

Dan Shomron had earlier focused the attention of his superiors by his devotion and talents. During the Six-Day War in 1967 he was appointed to command a paratroop force which operated recoilless guns mounted on jeeps and lay in cunning ambush for Egyptian tanks in northern Sinai. Shomron's force managed to knock out and destroy many of them, particularly 'Stalin's and 'T-54's, which fell one after another into the ambuscades Dan and his warriors set up for them.

The young officer – he was then only thirty years of age – and his paratroops were among the first to reach the Suez Canal on the fourth day of the Six-Day War in June 1967. For his resourcefulness, originality of conception and successful warfare he was awarded a commendation in despatches by the Chief of General Staff, Lieutenant-General Itzhak Rabin. A short while afterwards he was given the command of a regiment of paratroop regulars which took part in the 'war of attrition' and various expeditions.

From there he took up a temporary post on the General Staff. He preferred to remain in the field, where the action was, rather than occupy an office chair, even were it in the nerve-centre of army headquarters. But he realized then that his advancement depended upon a fundamental knowledge of the army in all its arms. Fortified by this realization, Dan took steps to further his professional specialization. He went through the Army Staff Command College, took an armour officers' course and even managed to study geography at Tel Aviv University. Upon the conclusion of his studies he was appointed officer commanding of the Armoured Brigade.

It was difficult for Shomron, a paratrooper to the core, to adapt to the strict and inflexible discipline imposed in the Armoured Corps. He was accustomed to what in the paratroop units was mainly an inner discipline and the informal, well-nigh free-and-easy relationship that exists between officers and other ranks. Moreover, his style of thought and action were still influenced by his service in the paratroop corps and were unacceptable to his new comrades in armour. But this trait did not detract from his effectiveness as a commander and the operational competence of his men, as had been demonstrated during the Yom Kipur War. Dan and his brigade took part in the battle that halted the Egyptian drive in their break-through to the Mitla Pass in Sinai, and even went to the assistance of the battered strongpoints along the Bar-Lev Line. Dan Shomron's brigade destroyed nearly sixty Egyptian tanks on the day of the great armour battle on 14 October 1973.

After the Day of Atonement War, Shomron was appointed to the general command of the Infantry and Paratroop division. The condition of his men was unsatisfactory to his way of thinking, both from the standpoint of their morale and of their outmoded equipment.

From that moment he set himself a goal – to restore the infantry, the 'footsloggers' in the British army term, to their old glory and self-confidence. He insisted upon up-to-date weaponry, means of high mobility transportation and means of active combat, so that they could have a decisive effect on the battlefield, and also other equipment which had not yet been seen in the corps.

Shomron fought for these objectives unremittingly. Most of his ideas and concepts were adopted, others were turned down because of limited funds which dictated a lower place on the scale of priorities. But his unwearied efforts to secure the improvement of the corps, his disregard of stagnant conservatism and his original ideas won the sympathy and appreciation of his commanders and men alike.

When the time came Dan Shomron was regarded by the top-level officers of the Army General Staff as the most suitable person to head the Entebbe rescue mission.

Shomron knew that, in spite of the risks, the prospects of success were good. His men trained and rehearsed in anticipation of the action for several days on a model of Entebbe Airport. It was so exact to the last detail that the way the doors opened in the simulated terminal building was faithfully replicated.

The exercises went on with dogged perseverance, constantly polishing up the techniques and results until the Brigadier-General was satisfied and certain that his men could accomplish their mission to the highest degree.

Part of the deployment of the units was undertaken even before the central government in Jerusalem had reached its final decision, with the ability to discontinue these moves at any moment. When the authorization came through the officers in charge could hardly believe their ears and their joy was boundless.

The order to the forces to begin to be 'at the ready' came on Thursday and from then on, as the Chief of General Staff declared, 'the cart was pushed forward'. Yoni Netanyahu made sure that, in his unit, the strike force, only the élite fighters should be included. Before the action, he carried out innumerable exercises and obdurately entered into even the smallest detail during the performance on the simulator. He continually reiterated to his men the maxim, which became part of their life, 'You learn from mistakes'.

During one of the briefings, before the action, Yoni added, 'Apart from all that I've told you, in the final event every one of you must use his common sense'.

With his wealth of experience in these exploits, Jonathan knew that during the fleeting seconds of a strike the conditions could change in the twinkling of an eye, and then everyone had to act with the utmost flexibility.

Upon the eve of the action the Minister of Defence met with the men and asked them if they felt they were ready. He asked them to answer 'with hand upon heart'. All of them, as one, chorused an affirmative.

The Minister, too, felt at peace with himself that he had seen the men off to the aircraft that were to take them to Entebbe. He knew that, if they had not gone, the catastrophe would have been immeasurable. The prestige of Israel would have sunk to the depths in the world's regard. What had happened in Uganda might encourage other African states to pursue the same course.

He prayed in his heart for the welfare of the youngsters who had gone out on their dangerous errand. He cherished full confidence that they would succeed. No one could have sent them out on that adventure without believing in their ability to deal with it. He knew that the Chief of Staff felt the same way as he did.

The operation as a whole might have been utterly wrecked had the hijackers at Entebbe paid attention to an item which appeared in the German paper *Abend-Zeitung* of Munich on Friday, 2 July:

'Paris – *Abend-Zeitung* service:

DRAMATIC TURN IN THE AFFAIR OF THE CAPTIVES
AT ENTEBBE

With the aim of gaining time, Israel has proposed to the aerial terrorists the opening of negotiations. As a result, the terrorists have postponed their ultimatum to Sunday noon. Diplomatic circles in Cairo now believe that Israel wants to despatch a commando unit to Uganda in order to rescue the captives in a daring operation.'

The report was evidently regarded as unreliable, if noted at all, and no one ascribed any importance to it in the belief that it was a 'journalistic canard'.

Entebbe. Saturday.

After his return from Mauritius, where he attended the Organisation of African Unity session, Idi Amin went to visit his 'guests'.

'The problems haven't been settled but there's some advance in the negotiations', he told the captives. 'We'll get another report tonight.'

The hostages had the impression that agreement had in effect been reached and there was an understanding with

Israel, but that Idi Amin wanted to bring television teams and the press the next morning to 'cover' the event and was consequently adjourning the liberation so that the communications media could have a field day.

The President had repeatedly mentioned his friend Colonel Bar-Lev to the Israelis and said, 'Tell him how well I treated you, and how I looked after you'.

Nonetheless, some of the hostages were worried that if Israel sent the requested terrorists to Uganda, who would guarantee their release by the gunmen?

When Boese, the German gang leader, was asked the question, he replied, 'We observe fair play'.

Someone asked if it had been fair play to hijack the aircraft, and he rejoined, 'You've got to distinguish between a hijacking and negotiations to settle the matter'.

For reasons of field security, censorship has prohibited the publication of the number of troops employed in 'Operation Jonathan' (The official name given to the raid by the Israeli Government).

But it is clear, as was said also by the Prime Minister, that the force that was deployed at Entebbe had not been created a week or two weeks prior to the action. It had taken years of effort, faith and devotion to the objective. The men came from different regular units. There were infantrymen, paratroopers and men of the Golani Brigade, and they reflected the average standard of the Israel Defence Force in its totality. Their competence stemmed from arduous preparation carried out quietly over the years without fuss or clamour, but with determination and responsibility.

Dan Shomron, as stated, was in over-all charge of the ground operation. The strike force was commanded by Lieutenant-Colonel Jonathan Netanyahu. At the 'intermediate stations' were the Chief of Operations Branch on the General Staff, Major-General Yekutiel Adam, and the commander of the Air Force, Major-General Benjamin Peled, who were in general command and reported to the Chief of Staff.

It is to be surmised that the term 'intermediate stations' which the Chief of Staff used, referred to the aircraft which served as flying command posts and as transmitting stations. The flight teams were not specially chosen and assigned by regular rota on the squadron's shift-schedule. In addition to these, participating units had been allocated by the Signals and Electronics Corps, the Medical Corps, the Israel Defence Force Maintenance set-up and of course men of the Intelligence Corps and the entire intelligence community.

7 The Liberators

When the Ministers assembled in the government meeting chamber in Tel Aviv raised their hands in token of 'Aye', the Chief of General Staff left at a run and ordered the start of the action.

The forces awaited the take-off command. Everything needed for the enterprise – arms, ammunition, jeeps and anti-tank carriers, sabotage equipment, medical equipment and signals equipment – were already stacked in the aircraft.

The planes themselves, the 'Hercules'-type (otherwise known to the world as 'Lockheed S-130'), were laden to capacity; six inner tanks were filled with jet aviation fuel that had been pumped into them up to the brim. Each 'Hercules' craft had two more giant outer tanks under the wings, each of them carrying 5,000 litres (approximately 1,000 gallons) of fuel.

These, then, were the aircraft on the wings of which the liberators would reach the victims of the hijackers at Entebbe. The Israel Air Force is said to have twenty-four of the planes which had been supplied by the Lockheed Company under contract approved by the United States' administration.

When the first of the 'Hercules' planes were delivered by Lockheed to the Israel Air Force, the local press stated that they were military transport planes with a range sufficient to reach from Israel to any destination in the Middle East. As a piquant feature the aviation correspondents noted that the 'Hercules' could even reach Burma, Siberia, South Africa and Iceland owing to its wide flight range. 'But', civilians then remarked, 'who wants to go to Africa at all?'

The flight teams of the first 'Hercules' aircraft in the Israel Air Force learned their initial operational lesson in sky warfare during the 1973 Yom Kipur campaign, like children thrown into the water in order to teach them to swim.

The teams to whom the mission to Uganda had been entrusted could be regarded as the carriers of the splendid tradition of the first air transport crews of the Air Force during the War of Liberation in 1948.

The 'Hercules' newcomers took part at the outset of the October 1973 war in the tremendous operation of flying thousands of men from the centre of the country to the battle areas. These modern craft, with the large 'windmills' at the extremity of the turbo-prop motors, ferried supplies and troops to the fronts, and on their return brought the wounded to hospitals in the centre of Israel.

More than once, while loaded to capacity, they ploughed through areas in which aerial dogfights were going on between Israeli 'Phantoms' and 'Mirages' against enemy planes, but the pilots of the big 'boats' were skilled enough to manoeuvre out of the battle zones. During that war, ground fire was directed at the 'Hercules' but none was hit.

A 'Hercules' captain once confidently told a newsman that his plane was capable of flying under no-visibility conditions and in any kind of weather from the North Pole to the Equator. The young pilot had made an unwitting prophecy because Entebbe, for which he was now bound, was only a few kilometres from the Equator, which crossed through Lake Victoria.

The navigation of the 'Hercules' was manipulated by an array of sophisticated systems unavailable in other Israel Air Force transport planes and which are mounted only in modern American fighter-planes. Radar screens stand before the navigator and the pilots. By using Radar and modern navigation instruments, 'Hercules' pilots are able to undertake complicated night flights which are out of the reach of other transport aircraft.

An instance of the Radar efficiency of the 'Hercules' was displayed when the Israeli submarine *Dakar* disappeared on a cruise some years ago. The aerial search over a certain area of the sea went on continuously for eight hours. Had the Israel Air Force then had 'Hercules' planes it would have been possible to reduce the length of the search to two hours.

It has been said that the 'Hercules' was the plane of the sixties to which the improvements and up-to-date embellishments have turned it into the outstanding airborne vessel of the seventies.

There would be no space to list all the countries in which the 'Hercules' jumbos have been added to their aerial establishments. Israel is not the only country in the Middle East which has received this plane. They also serve in the air forces of Abu Dhabi, Jordan, Kuwait and Saudi Arabia, one of whose planes entered Israel air space at the beginning of this year and was forced by Israeli fighters to land at Lod airport as an involuntary guest.

The planning officers at Israel Air Force headquarters naturally had the characteristics and advantages of the 'Hercules' in mind, for example, its ability to land on abbreviated runways only several hundred yards long. The range of the 'Hercules', about 4,000 km when loaded to maximum volume, presented no obstacle. Its large belly accommodates ninety-two soldiers or sixty-four paratroops fully equipped. When necessary it can carry seventy-four wounded men on stretchers in addition to two medical orderlies. The cabin is adapted to fly heavy military equipment, such as anti-tank gun-carriers, jeeps and even artillery. The loading ladder in its stern, with its immediate opening ability, provides a ramp down which vehicles or soldiers can get to the ground.

The moustached 'Hercules' pilot standing near his jumbo aircraft told the men who were shortly to be his flight passengers, 'Boys, this is a big ship but its flight characteristics are as easy to manage as any small aircraft.

Its manoeuvrability is considerable and it enables us to carry out fast manoeuvres. The wheels are pleasant to handle, the motors are superb and they respond excellently.'

'To sum up', the airman told the earthmen, 'I can warrant you that it can go down lower than any other transport plane without decreasing speed, and its night navigation is accurate without any problems.'

The flight teams knew they were about to take part in the most difficult and longest rescue operation ever undertaken by an air force. They were aware of the crucial role of the soldier. The airmen, caressing the three 'Hercules' craft with their glances, remembered that Israeli pilots had sat with Ugandan cadet learners at Entebbe Airport five years earlier and listened courteously to the President of Uganda who was addressing a flight graduation ceremony at the end of a course given by Israeli instructors.

Now, as the sun was about to set far over the mountains, they were on their way to rescue their brethren languishing at Entebbe from the hands of that same President who had so lavishly praised the skills and daring of the pilots of the Israel Air Force.

As the last hurried preparations for the mission of deliverance were being completed in faraway Israel, the captives at Entebbe had established a sort of communal existence. They had arranged turns among themselves to serve meals, carry out hygienic functions and tend to the sick. They had also invented various games, apart from bridge, which afforded relief in the long hours of boring captivity.

A piece of cardboard found lying around had been squared off as a draughts-board, and bottle-caps served as black and white draughts.

Cultural life was not neglected. An Israeli who knew Uganda from the time when he had served as an advisory expert there delivered a first-class lecture on the 'host country'. One of the French aircrew, a flight engineer by profession, described the air-bus.

They even once had the privilege of a shower, and thereafter the dingy hall in which they were held captive earned the sobriquet of 'Hilton Kampala'.

The children played quietly, but there was no laughter from them and sadness could be seen in their eyes.

Yoni's fighters, the men of the strike force, who were scheduled to be the vanguard to land on the runway at Entebbe, listened to the last briefing from their commander.

He went over and repeated the actions to be performed, and made certain that each one of them (the number of whom was astonishingly small) remembered his particular job.

Finally he summed up:

'It's clear that there'll be casualties. It's important that every one of you should remember that regardless of who will be hit, the break-in must be carried on without waiting to look after the wounded.

We've got to get in there, wipe out the terrorists and finish the job down to the last. We mustn't stop for a second until the hostages are safe.'

The seasoned warriors listened quietly to the briefing. They knew Yoni could be relied upon; the fact that he was leading them instilled confidence.

It was no accident that everyone depended on Yoni. The Israel Defence Force know that 'one could count on Yoni's word'. The almost legendary name of Lieutenant-Colonel

Jonathan Netanyahu had surfaced in the course of innumerable military exploits in which he had participated in his eleven-year army career.

To compare him as a military commander of the James Bond type was inane, as those who were intimately acquainted with him averred. They knew that Yoni was not a military officer who 'craved' battle and threw himself into the thick of danger because of an adventurous inclination. His judgement was cool and precise. He was endowed also with the ability to instil into each of his men the awareness of the just cause for which they were fighting, and the desire to give all; and in these lay his great qualities as a commander of men.

The thirty-year-old Yoni, a handsome and well-built man, of a refined masculine appearance, was born in the United States and was brought to Israel as an infant of two years old. His father, Professor Benzion Netanyahu, was editor-in-chief of the *Encyclopaedia Hebraica* in Jerusalem and had been on a Zionist mission in the United States until shortly after his eldest son, Jonathan, was born. He then returned to Israel and took up work there.

After long service in an infantry unit in the Israel Defence Force, Yoni served for a year as a battalion commander in the Armoured Corps. He then returned to his former unit, the same unit with whom he would later go on the mission to Uganda. He had a unique approach to his men. He sought many attributes in them, but one in particular stands out. One of his friends met him while he was training his men. To test them, Yoni first took them to rocky heights in the hills and asked them to descend and ascend a number of times. After they were thoroughly exhausted, he had them climb a long rope as many times as they could. He knew that there were some who were better than others in rope-climbing because they were stronger and better trained. But these were not necessarily the ones he wanted.

He wanted those lads who had exerted themselves to the last of their strength, regardless of the number of times they climbed the rope.

Physical ability, Yoni explained, could be achieved later through training; his foremost consideration was the will-power and perseverance of his future soldiers.

Friends who met him quite by chance a few weeks before the Entebbe operation said that he had not given up his ambition to complete his university studies while continuing army service. Those studies at Harvard University in the United States where Yoni excelled were twice interrupted because he felt that the army and his country needed him. While he dedicated the bulk of his adult life to the army, he nevertheless felt a strong desire to further develop his intellect in an academic setting.

The senior officers who decided to put Yoni in charge of the spearhead force knew that he had a brilliant military career ahead of him. Everyone recognized the fact that this young man was moulded of the same material from which the Chiefs of the Israel General Staff were fashioned.

The fighting men, for their part, felt only this: 'If Yoni goes with us there's no fear of defeat'.

The three jumbo-sized planes, loaded down to the last pound, took to the air one after another into the sunset, hugging the runway with their wheels until it seemed that they would never rise into the air.

But finally their broad wings went up in a tremendous roar of the motors and began the long haul to Entebbe. 'Operation Jonathan' was on the way.

The aircraft turned south-south-east along the Red Sea, following the route taken by civilian aircraft bound for South Africa, flying at a considerable height and trying not to draw the attention of the invisible waves groping like long fingers at them from the Radar posts installed by the Russians at Berbera in Somalia (where they operate apparently under Soviet control) and by the French at Djibuti, in French Somaliland.

There was no guarantee that during the long flight (over 4,000 km, approximately 2,500 miles) the 'Hercules' craft would not be detected by Radar stations *en route*, but it was hoped they would be identified as ordinary civilian passenger planes making their way south along this air-path.

The flight to Entebbe was made in fluctuating weather conditions and they encountered storms which compelled them to by-pass these disturbances and change the original course. The guesses made by different newsmen that the Israeli planes pretended to be civilian aircraft and kept in wireless contact with control stations on the way were unfounded. The 'model' flight, taken by the Chief of General Staff on the eve of the operation, proved that the Israeli planes were capable of functioning without assistance from the ground.

At about one-third of the journey the planes veered south, crossed the coastline and turned into Africa, over Ethiopia, on their way to the frontier of Kenya. Until that point, while they were invisible to the eyes of the people in the 'Hercules' aircraft, an observant eye and mailed fist watched over them in the shape of 'F-45 Phantom' aircraft emblazoned with the blue Shield of David of the Israel Air Force.

These precautions were rendered necessary by the fact that the unarmed transport planes were flying in dangerous proximity to hostile Arab countries, especially Egypt and Saudi Arabia. But when the fighter-planes reached the end of their cruising range, they made a wide turn and returned to their base in Israel.*

* It would of course have been possible to extend the range of the fighter-planes by fuelling in flight from flying tankers which are in the service of the Israel Air Force, but it was decided to dispense with this possibility.

The Hercules planes continued on their path along the full length of Ethiopia, still undetected and still not encountering opposition.

6 p.m. The Prime Minister and Foreign Minister are in the Operations Room of the Ministry of Defence, their entire attention concentrated on the forces flying on now for two hours. Their thoughts are wholly focused on the hope that the liberators will succeed in reaching Entebbe with complete surprise.

Meanwhile, telephone connection has been established with the Israeli Ambassador in Paris. The conversation continues for about half-an-hour. The talk pivots around the 'exchange of hostages for imprisoned terrorists'.

No new developments are reported from the other side. The gunmen at Entebbe Airport have again hardened their attitude and Idi Amin is pressuring Israel to surrender unconditionally.

The Ministers know that the colloquy is being eavesdropped, but even at this moment they are not inclined to be distracted from the objective. If the field at Entebbe is found to be blocked, then the Hercules aircraft will have to return, and then there will be no alternative other than to resume the fatiguing negotiations, in which the prospects of success seem so faint.

Shimon Peres at that time faced a dilemma. He had been invited to a Bar Mitzvah (confirmation) ceremony which was to be held in those very critical hours when the Hercules aircraft were cleaving the skies of Africa on their way to Entebbe.

If he failed to turn up at the reception, Peres feared, people might sense that something important was going on. Consequently, he decided to go, and strode off from the Defence Ministry in the Tel Aviv Kirya to the Bar Mitzvah party. When he appeared he was encircled by the newsmen present and asked for details of what was happening.

His well-known smile wreathing his lips (and the best-kept secret at the moment in the State of Israel locked up tightly inside him) the Minister said,

'I believe it will all be over within twenty-four hours . . .'

Another guest at the reception was Knesset-member, Menahem Begin, the Opposition leader, who was, as we know, privy to the secret. He maintained an impassive expression and revealed no trace of the feelings seething within him. But when he met the Chief Rabbi of the Israel Defence Forces, Major-General Mordecai Piron, he decided that he had to disclose the secret to him.

He asked the Rabbi to go with him into a corner where, in whispered undertones, he revealed that in those very moments Israel Defence Force soldiers were winging their way, as eagles, to rescue the captives.

The cleric took out of his pocket a small sheet of paper bearing the caption, 'Prayer for a Journey by Air', and both of them recited the verses with profound devotion:

'May it please the Almighty God of our Fathers, Who has placed the clouds over the chariots that move on the wings of the spirit, to bear in safety and lead in peace and bring to the home of our desires, for life and gladness and peace, and save us from the hand of all our enemies and those who lie in wait for us in the heavens and on earth, and from the spirits that are evil and from all manner of hazards in flying through the air and from wickedness and all kinds of iniquity that threaten to appear. And may we be given His mercy and compassion in His eyes and the eyes of all who look upon us. And so may Thou hear in the heavens the prayer of Thy nation, Israel, in loving kindness. Blessed be Thou, O Lord, who giveth heed to prayer, that His angels protect and preserve Thee in all the ways.'

Entebbe. Saturday noon. The young lad, Bennie Davidson, had said that, in his opinion, soldiers of the Israel Defence

Force would come to liberate the captives at midnight. Those who heard him just smiled. But Bennie really meant what he said.

'Do you know what the distance is between Israel and Uganda?' he was asked.

'Of course I know!' he rejoined, adding, 'if it weren't so far, the soldiers would have been here by now.'

Most of the hostages had no strength left to smile. They had been suffering from strong stomach pains since the morning and many of them had been vomiting. It appeared that the malady which had overcome them originated with the filthy meat they had been eating, as the pious Jews who had not tasted the viands were not afflicted.

The water in the taps had run out, the services were fetid and the sanitary conditions could be no worse. Physical weakness, coupled with the report that the negotiations had apparently broken down and that the terrorists were threatening to execute them the next day, had engendered an atmosphere of black despair.

The threat was becoming more and more potent before their eyes. The airport employees had parked the air-bus (which until then had been stationed some distance from the spot) outside the terminal itself. The rumour spread that the gunmen had booby-trapped it and were prepared to explode it the next day simultaneously with the blowing up of the terminal building in which the hostages were being held.

Towards evening the President of Uganda paid another visit. He had just returned from the conference in Mauritius in his private plane (a double-jet 'Westwind' made by Israel Aircraft Industries, for which he had never paid).

He was full of praise for the hijackers. They repeated that all his efforts to save the hostages would be fruitless unless Israel complied with the gunmen's demands in full.

'Big Daddy' wore the bright blue uniform of a Marshal of the Ugandan Air Force, that same establishment the foundations of which had been laid by Israeli pilots and technicians.

The Ugandan Air Force had started out as a small air arm which had been engaged mainly on police patrols. The flight instructors, technical officers and aircraft mechanics who had been sent from Israel laid the bases for a modern aerial force. They trained the Ugandan air cadets in 'Fouga Magister' craft. The Ugandan Air Force had depended on the Israelis alone for a number of years, but then, some time before the Yom Kipur War, they started to draw closer to the U.S.S.R. which provided them with lavish grants.

Idi Amin had tried, since his advent to power, to create a powerful air force through which he could foist his will on the countries neighbouring his own, especially Kenya which he constantly menaced.

The Ugandan Air Force, towards whose air space the 'Hercules' jumbos were approaching, was not as small as people thought. It had ten of the most modern fighters of the 'MiG-21' type, fifteen years old but still effective, attack aircraft of the 'MiG-17' class and eight 'Fouga Magister' planes of those which had been brought in at the time by the Israelis and were left behind on their departure. These planes served at one and the same time for training and light attack purposes. 'Arrow-29' planes, made in Czechoslovakia, were also used as trainers, as were two-seater 'MiG-15's and some light Italian aircraft. The Ugandan Air Force establishment also possessed six 'Dakota' transport planes, eleven Italian-made helicopters and ten light liaison and reconnaissance craft of the 'Piper' class.

Intelligence reports which had reached Israel brought the assurance that the Ugandan air machines constituted no source of worry to the 'Hercules' jumbos. The Ugandan planes were in large part under repair and constantly being checked out, and their pilots were of such a low order of skill that even Idi Amin Dada was afraid to fly with them.

Yet all that has been said above was no obstacle to the Palestine Liberation Organization when it reached agreement with Idi Amin to train Palestinians to fly his planes as part of the Ugandan Air Force. After having gone through various stages of aerial training, Idi Amin convened his Palestinian cadets one day towards the end of 1975 and delivered a sermon to them in the style of which he was so fond.

'You are called upon to get ready here for the main invasion of Palestine', he told the assembled air trainees. 'You must not only be ready to fight the enemy yourselves, but all the countries aiming at liberating Palestine, with Uganda at their head, will be with you ... As long as you are here, you must regard yourselves as being in your homeland and alongside your brothers in battle serving in the Ugandan Air Force.'

An official announcement about the agreement was issued by the Palestine Liberation Organization offices in Beirut in August 1975. Naturally it did not specify what kind of 'military assistance' was meant, and for what purposes, but these facts were clarified through the sentiments expressed by Idi Amin himself to the Palestinian Arabs. 'Abu 'Amar told me personally that while you are staying here, you are under my direct command, and I am therefore entitled to give you every mission which is connected with the interest of Arab Palestine or Africa.'

It would seem, then, that both parties derive mutual advantage from the agreement which is no different in substance from Palestine Liberation Organization arrangements with various organizations, except that this time it was concluded with a State, and not an organization.

Idi Amin uses the Palestinian Arabs under his command (apart from the cadet pilots there are 400 Palestinian Arabs in his territory) for sabotage actions in African countries, and they also constitute his personal bodyguard. Just as he once relied upon the Israelis more than on his own country-men, so now he depends on the Palestinian Arabs to protect him from his own Ugandan bodyguards.

The reward given to the Palestinian Arabs was made evident in the French plane-snatch. 'The Arab states are not happy to train our pilots', Amin was told by 'Abu Gabara', a Palestinian terrorist leader, 'But you, General, have done for the Palestinians what their brothers refused to do!'

Uganda Radio announced in October 1975 'arduous exercises', 'a suicide squadron' of Palestinian and Ugandans in the Nayogabo district of southern Uganda. The Ugandan aviation authorities even warned civilian pilots not to come too close to the zone of the manoeuvres until further notice.

The operational standard of the Palestinian Arab airmen (and even those of their Ugandan instructors) may be gathered from the frequent reports about accidents in the Air Force there. Over the past year the press have published a number of reports on Ugandan planes which crashed during training. Among those killed in these mishaps was a twenty-nine-year-old Palestinian Arab pilot known as 'George', but whose real name was Yussef Baragit, who lost his life when his plane crashed in Uganda on 29 October 1975. The man joined the 'Fatah' organization in 1967 and was appointed commander of 'the suicide squadron' consisting of Palestinian Arabs after having undergone training in China and Algeria from 1968 to 1970.

8   The Rescue

Over Ethiopia one of the unit's officers in the first 'Hercules' rose and sat beside Yoni. The young man was intimately acquainted with his senior and had a nagging feeling that he was going to be hurt.

Finally he plucked up courage and said earnestly, 'Yoni, be careful. Don't forget you're in command – you mustn't be hit'.

The other smiled and returned a curt, 'I understand.'

But it was clear to the young subaltern that Yoni was concerned with other matters. As the one directing the raid he would have to race ahead of his men and position himself at the centre of action in order to get a total picture of the situation from the outset.

Dan Shomron and Yoni sat beside each other in quiet discussion. The aircraft would soon be landing at Entebbe. Yoni returned to his own seat and in high spirits exchanged a few last words with his lads, shook hands with the men and officers at his side and imbued them with his own faith and calm confidence.

The flight of the 'Hercules' aircraft neared the frontier of Kenya. On this leg of the journey they went down to a lower altitude so that they could come in under the Radar beams from Uganda. Close to the target area they ran into low cloud and stormy air conditions. Nevertheless, the navigation had been pin-pointedly accurate. The first plane was due to arrive at Entebbe on the minute.

Several minutes before midnight, as had been the case every

night in Entebbe, Lizette Haddad washed the only garments in her possession: the suit she had worn on leaving Lod Airport in Israel and her husband's and her own underwear. She lay down to sleep in a bikini swimsuit which had by chance been in her handbag.

Another captive, Dr Michael ('Misha') Rabinowitz, thought of his three children left behind in Israel with relatives and grieved that he would never see them again. He felt he ought to write to his relatives and hoped the Ugandans would display a humanitarian attitude and agree to mail the letter, if he were killed by the gunmen.

Under the vigilant eyes of the soldiers Misha wrote: 'Be brave and look after the education of the children. I know it will be difficult – but that is my last request'.

He handed the letter to a Ugandan soldier and asked him to mail it to France. The man took the letter, turned it over hesitatingly but in the end agreed to Dr Rabinowitz's request.

The payment he asked for and received was the physician's gold cigarette lighter.

The scene in the old terminal passenger hall was no different from other nights. The hundred-and-nine captives were scattered in various corners. Some of them had stretched out on the mattresses on the floor and tried to doze off, in spite of their diarrhoea and stomach pains. Others were sitting and playing one of their interminable card-games to while away the time and forget their anxieties.

Wilfred Boese and the German terrorist woman (whom everyone called 'The Nazi bitch') stood on guard at the entrance to the building. Two other gunmen, one of whom was Faiz al Jaber, stood sentry in the hall, Kalatchnikoff rifles in hand. Three more gunmen were resting in the small rooms adjoining the hall.

The descent to the old 2,400 metre runway at Entebbe was

swift and they taxied up to the field in moonlight, which illuminated the waters of nearby Lake Victoria with a silver radiance.

The pilots' had avoided using the new runway, 3,700 metres in length, which had been laid down some years back by the Israeli 'Solel Boneh' public works combine, owing to the distance from the terminal building in which the hostages were being held.

The Radar personnel should have spotted the aerial intruders but for some reason failed to do so. It can only be surmised that their vigilance was at a low ebb because the next plane due to arrive, a regular flight of East African Airways, was not expected for another couple of hours. Another supposition, advanced by electronic experts, is that one of the Israeli planes had Radar-blocking devices which slightly smudged the arrival of the planes off the control tower Radar screen.

But whatever the reason, the four tower employees were due to pay with their lives for what Idi Amin regarded as a fatal shortcoming.

During that time another Israeli plane, a Boeing 707, cruised around in the skies over Entebbe. It served as the aerial transmitting-station which maintained the contact between the commanders of the ground action and the War Room at General Headquarters back in Tel Aviv. (There is a supposition that Generals Adam and Peled were in this plane.)

Another 'Boeing' plane had landed earlier at Nairobi airport in neighbouring Kenya. It was fitted out as a flying hospital and there were twenty-three doctors and two fully-equipped operating rooms standing by on board. The planners of the rescue action had feared there might be a large number of casualties and to counter this possibility made all the necessary preparations to save lives.

The wheels of the first 'Hercules' touched down on the lit-up runway at Entebbe one minute after midnight, precisely according to plan. Dan Shomron sighed with relief. He knew that if the landing went off well, there was every prospect that the action as a whole would succeed. He exchanged an encouraging glance with Yoni prior to the sortie.

From the moment the wheels of the first 'Hercules' carrying Yoni and his assault force kissed the tarmac only a few seconds elapsed before they were on their way to the terminal. Dan Shomron stayed behind to await the arrival of his auxiliary forces which would later fan out in other parts of the airport.

The raiders roared forward in the vehicles they had brought along in the belly of the plane, their entire thoughts concentrated upon one sole objective – to get to the terminal building before the guards realized what was happening.

There were only a few fateful seconds available to them until the guards recovered their wits, and it was during that brief interval that the fate of the hostages would be determined.

The pilots gazed with incredulity at the speed with which the strike force erupted down the landing hoist in the tail onto the ground. They had never in their lives witnessed such a swift *glissando* of movement. They stood open-mouthed.

The second 'Hercules', too, landed not far from the terminal structure.

Within a few moments a heavy exchange of firing was being waged. The Ugandans switched off the electric power, and the last of the trio of 'Hercules' aircraft was compelled to land by moonlight, as the verge beacons on the runway were darkened.

Some ten yards before the terminal building Yoni and his foremost commandos ran into the first sentry and Yoni tackled and wiped him out. Immediately after this a second Ugandan sentry was encountered and he too was expeditiously dealt with.

Now the strike force was beside the long, low terminal building and they fanned out. A terrorist standing outside was hit in one of his legs, retreated and managed to run outside.

Within seconds the invaders were lined up at the entrance and burst in simultaneously through the main entrance and the large windows.

Another squad stormed into the hall through the services rooms, while a third raced forward and took up covering positions at the side of the building.

The fighters who had burst into the hall shouted warnings in Hebrew to the captives to lie on the ground and they then wiped out the Palestinian Arab terrorists in the hall within a few seconds with crackling volleys of automatic fire.

The fierce combat raged as the captives lay prone on the floor between the Israel Defence Force commandos and the terrorists, and the bullets whizzed in trajectories the length of the hall.

Those who hugged the floor were not hit. The terrorists had not had time to hurl grenades at the soldiers or the hostages.

During a brief lull in the firing Wilfred Boese returned suddenly to the passenger hall. It had been his intention to fulfil the threat made by the terrorists to mow down most of the people inside.

Ilan Har-Tuv, the forty-eight-year-old Israeli economist, eldest son of Dora Bloch, watched with alarm how the German turned swiftly on his heels and pointed his automatic weapon at dozens of unfortunate hostages lying prone on the ground.

But Boese was in a panic. With the same rapidity that he had burst into the hall he swivelled round again, ran outside and opened fire into the darkness. That very same moment he was hit by raking fire and went down lifeless together with his German female companion.

Within forty-five seconds the four terrorists who were the greatest menace to the hostages had been wiped out. That was in effect the moment of liberation for the captives, although many hazards were still to be expected.

Yoni had stayed in front of the building when his main squad dashed in. He wanted to be nearest to it, yet able to control his other squads surrounding the terminal in case Ugandan forces were to interfere from different directions. Also, one of the problems encountered during the planning stage involved the enemy who were located on the second floor of the terminal. There was a reserve of nearly sixty soldiers of the Ugandan army upstairs (many of them trained by Israeli instructors in past years).

When the commandos stormed the second floor there were no longer sixty men there as the majority had fled. But twenty or so were still left, and these were killed during a brief battle.

Apart from the four terrorists wiped out in the initial assault, three more were mopped up in the room where they were resting during a parallel action. The seven terrorists were able to fire only a few rounds before they perished.

The passenger hall was swirling with smoke and dust. Several blankets had begun to burn and the smoke rose in a thick column. Flakes of plaster drifted from the ceiling and walls, and the acrid stench of gunpowder penetrated the nostrils. Eyes smarted and throats were stung into fits of coughing.

Several minutes more elapsed inside the hall before the Israel Defence Force troops quelled the sources of the firing, which came mainly from neighbouring structures and the second floor of the terminal building. The orders were to direct fire at the sources of firing and the fighters carried out these instructions until the fighting ceased.

Yoni had taken up position outside the entrance to the terminal during the actual 'break-in', and it must be remembered that this took only seconds, in order to command and co-ordinate his squads.

As soon as the terrorists had been annihilated, and after the action in the ground-floor passenger hall was completed, fire was opened from the control tower. Yoni had not overlooked the tower in his planning and the danger implicit in it had worried him all the time.

The question that had exercised his mind was whether to deal with the Ugandans in the tower before the 'break-in'. It was evident to him that, were this to be done, it would rob the assault of the element of surprise. Nonetheless, he had prepared a squad to take on the tower personnel and his men were ordered to direct enfilading fire at the tower only at the moment when the first shots came from it.

Undoubtedly the Ugandans in the tower had binoculars. They focused on Yoni and became aware that he commanded the operation.

Although conscious of the danger, Yoni decided to take up his post in front of the terminal façade, exposed to possible fire from the tower, as he considered this essential to remaining in control of the action.

He had more than once said that one of the things which had to be done when you were in charge of an operation, in addition to shooting and running, was to stay with 'your head above', watching and directing everything going on in the field of action, and the spot he chose did in fact enable him to oversee the squads in action.

The squad instructed to direct covering fire at the control tower before it began to act of its own accord had so far not done so. Now fusillades were coming from the tower and other directions and Yoni's squads returned fire.

Yoni momentarily turned with his back to the tower. A bullet fired from it, pierced his back and penetrated to the heart. He fell to the ground and an army doctor rushed forward in order to tend him. With his last breath Yoni tried to rise and say something but the words were unintelligible.

Soldiers nearby rushed forward and carried him gently to the assault vehicle as the doctor continued to tend him. The eyes of the commando boys were moist with tears, but betrayed none of their inner grief: a bullet in the back had killed Yoni, as no one could have felled him face-to-face.

His men were not flustered. The second-in-command to Yoni at once took over. The covering force succeeded in that very moment in silencing the firing from the tower and the first of the hostages began to emerge from the doorway of the terminal to race to the awaiting aircraft.

The Chief of the General Staff in Israel, Lieutenant-General 'Motta' Gur, followed the course of the operation in the company of several aides. All those people who were involved in the decision at the political level, and in the execution of the plan at the military level, were sitting or standing in the office of the Defence Minister. A quasi-command post had been set up in the Minister's office from the early evening hours.

Among those sitting in his suite of offices in the Defence Ministry in the Tel Aviv Kirya during the crucial hours were Prime Minister Itzhak Rabin, Foreign Minister Yigal Allon, Trade and Commerce Minister Haim Bar-Lev, Transport Minister Gad Ya'acobi and several deputy Ministers and their advisers.

The statesmen listened intently to the reports coming in from the scene of action. The atmosphere was charged with tension that mounted until the moment it was announced that the action inside the terminal passenger hall had ended and the hostages were being evacuated.

Outside Israel itself the first report of the Israel Defence

Force rescue operation was recorded in the log-book of the emergency staff that had been working continuously in the Interior Ministry at Bonn, West Germany.

It was an abbreviated message from the German Ambassador at Kampala, capital of Uganda, Dr Richard Ellerkmann, over the open telephone line between the Embassy and the Ministry in Bonn.

The Ambassador reported, with excitement choking his voice, 'Two German citizens living near the Entebbe Airport have this moment reported that about fifteen minutes ago they heard shooting from the vicinity of the airport. A plane was also seen and it didn't stop its motors turning over after landing'.

The message was at once flashed to Chancellor Helmut Schmidt.

Another report that reached Germany from Kampala stated: 'The firing has been going on for forty minutes.' Five minutes later another report – 'One of the airport buildings is going up in flames.'

9 Back to Freedom

When the Israel Defence Force operation crashed into action Baruch Gross was the first of his family to hear the shots. His wife fell on top of their son and shielded him with her body.

Baruch raised himself slightly from the ground and looked outside. At that instant he saw the German terrorist being hit and, in the same split second, heard a voice yelling out in Hebrew.

Someone was calling to them to go outside. He picked up a thick mattress as a buffer against bullets, gathered up his wife and son and raced with them towards the vehicles standing outside the entrance.

The soldiers posted around the vehicles were returning fire while many of the passengers were struggling wildly towards them. It was a shocking moment. Other passengers decided to run to the plane and they arrived ahead of the vehicles.

The wounded and dead were loaded on the aircraft. Baruch tried to hide the sight of them from his son's eyes but the young lad saw everything.

At first, on hearing the shots, the thought flashed through Joseph Haddad's mind that the terrorists imprisoned in Israel had been brought to Entebbe and that it was they who were now firing. He took up a chair to cover his head when he saw the terrorists standing over them firing their weapons.

The terrorists outside had by then been liquidated, but Haddad and the other hostages knew nothing of this. One bullet hit the chair he was holding up. He was certain others would follow. The German terrorist leapt outside and suddenly Joseph Haddad saw him lying on the ground, in a pool of blood, and Israeli soldiers crowding into the hall. For a moment he was dumbfounded, everything was so confused and incomprehensible.

Then one of the commandos called out to them, '*Chevra*, folks, lie down, we're soldiers of Zahal – Israel Defence Force'.

Never in his life had he heard more wonderful words than these. His wife still could not take in what was happening. She was at first sure that the terrorists had come to liquidate them one-by-one. She covered her face in the blanket and rolled off the mattress on to the floor.

Joseph gasped at her, excitedly, 'Didn't you hear? They're ours! They told us, "*Chevra*, calm down, we're taking you, don't worry!" '

He gripped his wife's hand and they raced outside as the soldiers screened them like a living wall. They piled up with dozens of other liberated passengers on the command-car which sped them to the aircraft.

Before they ran out of the terminal building Lizette managed to snatch the slacks of her suit which she had washed and hung up to dry. She hoped to be able to dress somehow. Later she found that the pants had bullet-holes in them.

Emma Rosenkrantz, a resident of Jerusalem, had been lying beside her husband Claude and two children, ten-year-old son Noam and five-year-old daughter Ella, certain that the gunmen had come to shoot them all. But suddenly 'an angel from Heaven', to use her term, appeared inside the hall and called out in a quiet voice, 'I'm from Israel. Dress at once. We're taking you home'.

For Joseph Abugedir, the Israeli who had been suspicious of the date given to him by his seat-companion on the Air France plane a moment before he turned out to be an Arab Terrorist, the finest moment in that drama of liberation was on hearing the cry, 'Run directly to the plane. Without shoes. Quick! Quick!' He wanted to kiss the soldiers, but there was no time.

Sixteen-year-old Michal Warshavsky was awake when the commando unit raced into the hall. She had not heard the roar of the planes but suddenly heard the sound of shooting. She lay prostrate on the floor. Then, hearing the cry of '*Chevra*, you can get up', she knew that she was saved. She gazed with great love at the daring boys who had come so far to free her.

Mrs Davidson, too, had not heard the noise of the aircraft landing at Entebbe although she and her husband were not asleep at the time. Throughout their immurement in the terminal building they had slept usually no more than a few hours and had occupied their waking hours with a variety of games.

Eventually, when they had stretched out to sleep, they heard the shooting. Sarah, her husband and children rushed to the comfort rooms. It was evident that something terrible was going on. They also asked themselves, 'Have they perhaps come to kill us?' Sarah lay over her youngest son Bennie and cradled his head in her arms, while her husband protected the older boy Ron with his body.

Bennie, who was crushed between his mother and the floor, knew instinctively who the people were who had burst into the hall. He had been expecting them. Now he felt he had to pray. He had even composed a special prayer for himself and called it the 'Uganda Prayer'. But in the excitement of the moment he forgot the exact words.

His lips murmured, 'God ... God ... I beseech you, maybe Zahal soldiers have really come, then now, at the last moment, before we are saved, God, please, I beg you ...'

His mumbled words were cut off by a short, slight-figured soldier who burst into the building grasping a Kalatchnikoff rifle that looked bigger than himself. The dark-complexioned young man said something in Hebrew. Everything became amazingly clear. There was no need for further explanations. The Israel Defence Force had come to free them – all they had to do was to dash outside with this young man. They wanted to kiss and embrace him but were petrified by the stunning impact of the moment.

One of the hostages, Itzhak David, had been wounded when he tried to help Jean-Jacques Maimoni, who had been hit and killed during the first minutes of the assault. The bullet had entered Itzhak David's left shoulder and pierced his lung. Someone tried to bandage him and immediately afterwards he ran towards one of the 'Hercules' planes.

His friend, Dr Itzhak Hirsch, a paediatrician living at Kiryat Haim, a suburb of Haifa in northern Israel, tended him until the army doctors took over.

The first thought that darted into Rina Cooper's mind when she heard the shots was that perhaps the terrorists had broken down, perhaps they had lost patience and were going to wipe out the hostages. She lowered her head and whispered to her husband Yerach, 'Hold me!' The thoughts tumbled over each other in her mind as in a mad whirlpool, 'The bullets have already hit me, Enough! Enough!'

Cushions sailed through the air, an armchair caught fire, stones rattled to the floor.

Rina marvelled, 'Is this what battle is like? How can the lads stand it? It sends one crazy. Where can I hide? I wish it were all over!' Then, suddenly, she realized who was firing. It seemed like a miracle. Deep pride swelled in her heart for the wonderful boys who had gained control of the situation so quietly and confidently. But she still found it hard to comprehend in the first moments, 'Are these our soldiers here? In Uganda?'

The voice of a soldier, amplified by a megaphone he was carrying, reached her ears, 'We've come to take you home!'

Hard on his heels other men came in and asked the hostages to help them to identify the bodies of the dead terrorists. Suddenly three Ugandans came out, hands on their heads. The captives recognized them at once – these were the cleaners in the comfort rooms. They shouted at the soldiers, 'Don't hurt them. They're good. They looked after us'.

The soldiers let the trio run away.

As Brigadier-General Dan Shomron continued the over-all control operation from his command-post, he heard that one of the units was 'out of work'. These were the men who had been sent to the outer edges of the airport to repel any possible reinforcements that might come from the nearby Ugandan military camp. As far as was known there were some hundreds of troops garrisoned there.

Other forces had taken over the new terminal building at Entebbe and the control system of the flight tower. The occupation of the tower enabled the 'Hercules' aircraft to move across the runway, in accordance with pre-arranged instructions and planning, to the various points on the airport where they were necessary for the progress of the action.

The firing went on as the liberated captives, some fully clad and others in swim-suits or swathed only in blankets, were taken to the planes whose motors were still running.

The Israeli commandos stood at their control posts and returned whatever fire was directed at them by Ugandan soldiers.

A squad drawn from Yoni's strike force crossed to the line of 'MiG' fighters parked beside the terminal and destroyed eleven of them (seven 'MiG-21's and four 'MiG-17's) with bursts of fire, grenades and explosive charges.

Other Ugandan aircraft, including President Idi Amin's personal plane, the Westwind, standing some way off, were spared. The commando sappers had no time to deal with them. The men of Yoni's assault force who had assisted the hostages in evacuating the passenger hall noticed the difference between the behaviour of the Israelis and the passengers of other nationalities. The *sabras* did not wait for instructions during the moments of liberation; they knew what was expected of them and what to do. They rallied quickly from the initial shock and began to race across the tarmac to the planes.

One of the soldiers even found time to remark to a companion, 'They know that we didn't come on the wings of the *Shechinah* (holy spirit) alone'.

Men and women, young and middle-aged, stooped as they ran, with the bullets whistling above their heads from all sides, as if they had been in training for this kind of dash all their lives.

The non-Israelis, on the other hand, had to receive briefings, but nevertheless their conduct was exemplary and they did not lose their heads after the first moments of confusion.

'Will you come with us or do you want to stay here?' an Israeli officer asked the captain of the captured French airliner.

'For God's sake, take us with you!' exclaimed Captain Bacos, and joined with the rest of his aircrew and the hostages dashing to clamber on the 'Hercules' aircraft.

The evacuation of the freed passengers was conducted quietly and expeditiously. Most of them kept silent and followed in the tracks of their liberators, except for the wounded who were loaded on the vehicles with the doctors tending them and giving first aid.

Suddenly fire was opened up once more from the nearby tower, but the Israeli commandos responded with a concerted volley that silenced the attackers at once.

The operation had claimed a toll of four lives at Entebbe –

three civilians, Jean-Jacques Maimoni, Pasco Cohen and Ida Borowitz, and one of the military men, Lieutenant-Colonel Jonathan Netanyahu. Five civilians and four soldiers were wounded, one of the latter seriously. He had been shot by two Ugandan soldiers as he was storming the terminal building.

Ten army doctors, who arrived at Entebbe with the invading force, treated the wounded with the best of mobile medical equipment. The Army Medical Corps had foreseen every need down to the last detail. Thus, for example, doctors had brought with them jugs of milk and distilled water for passengers who were suffering from stomach ailments.

The large number of doctors who took part in 'Operation Jonathan' at Entebbe and Nairobi, thirty-three in all, bore out the possibility of heavy casualties that had been taken into account during the planning stage.

A particularly moving spectacle was the encounter between the aircrew personnel of the 'Hercules' transport plane and the passengers whom they helped up into the interior.

'I was so overcome with emotion when I met these people as they came on board', one of the young navigators confessed later, 'that I had tears in my eyes'.

Thousands of miles away from Entebbe, at General Headquarters, of the Israel Defence Force, the Chief of Staff and his senior officers overheard the drama that unfolded at the scene of action.

They had listened to almost every word exchanged in conversations among the units themselves and between the squads. Others who 'listened in' were Major-Generals Peled, the Air Force Commander, and Adam, the Chief of Operations Branch, who were in the intermediate station and who had caught every word that was uttered out of the communications equipment of the detachments deployed at Entebbe.

The excellent system of command and control which the Israel Defence Force possesses has been renowned for its superior quality for many years past. Overseas newspapers have stressed that, during the commando raid on Beirut to liquidate the terror organization headquarters, in April 1973, the General Headquarters in Israel heard every word said over the communications devices installed in the hired limousines in which the raiders were travelling, even at high speed, through the streets of the Lebanese capital.

The whole operation lasted only fifty-three minutes – two minutes less than the dress rehearsal held on the previous day in Israel.

Before the Israeli commandos left the terminal building, the walls of which were pockmarked by hundreds of bullets and in which pools of blood stained the tiled paving outside and the parquet flooring inside, they carefully located the bodies of the seven dead terrorists, the five Palestinian Arabs and the two Germans, male and female.

The documents found on the corpses were removed; they were photographed and their fingerprints taken with perfect finesse.

The identification process was carried out to assist the Israeli intelligence service and those of other countries in the world. The only ones to be identified were the German, Wilfred Boese, and the Arabs, Ja'il el-Arja and Faiz Abdul-Rahim Jaber. The German woman was not positively identified, but it is assumed she was Kroecher-Tiedmann.

Another of the terrorists escaped with his life because he was with President Idi Amin at the time of the Israeli incursion. He was the Peruvian anarchist, Antonio Bouvier, who was the leader of the terror group at Entebbe. The chance invitation to be at President Amin's palace that evening had saved his life.

After the former occupants of the terminal passenger-hall were safely on the 'Hercules', the French pilot, Captain Bacos, was approached by the Israeli pilot, who shook hands in comradely greeting and inquired if all the aircrew of the French air-bus were aboard the 'Hercules' plane and were alive and well.

Once assured of this, the Israel Air Force men proceeded to conduct a second tally of the freed passengers. With the correct total established, they pulled up the tail and when it was locked in place, the first of the 'Hercules' saviour aircraft took off on the long flight home to Israel.

Only one of the hostages, the seventy-four-year-old Dora Bloch, a charming old lady of dual Israeli and British nationality who had become a beloved figure among the Entebbe captives because of her kind heart and warm personality, was left behind in Uganda.

She had been taken by ambulance from Entebbe to a local hospital in Kampala on the Thursday when some meat had lodged in her throat and the doctor among the hostages had advised medical treatment.

Dora Bloch was never to be seen by her family and friends in Europe and America again. After the coup at Entebbe, she was murdered there and her body was not recovered for decent burial in Israel.

10 Aftermath

With the evacuation of the freed passengers, the commanders on the spot decided to leave without further delay.

It had not been possible to refuel at Entebbe with enough speed and it was consequently decided, as the Chief of the General Staff stated later at a press conference in Tel Aviv, to 'foist' themselves on Kenya for a fuelling stop.

Owing to the cramped space on board the aircraft, which was crammed with liberated people, the fuel-pumps were left behind at Entebbe.

Immediately after the aircraft had taken to the air from Entebbe, the local communications network was completely dislocated. The magazine *Aviation Week* believed that this was the result of the use of some sort of interference devices on board the 'Hercules' intruders, which, as the weekly added, carried highly sophisticated electronic combat instruments.

There was another 'plum' pulled out of the aerial 'grab' and displayed in the world press – before their departure, the Israeli invaders planted delayed-action bombs throughout the airport at Entebbe, and the sound of explosions were heard for many hours, long after the Israeli aircraft were winging their way on an advanced leg of the journey back.

The tired civilian passengers sat in the military plane, at the other end of which stretchers were ranged. None of them voiced any joy. There were casualties, dead, wounded. The oppressive fatigue of the gruelling days of captivity now overcame the former hostages. Some lay back and closed their eyes, sleeping amid the commotion, the roar of the engines and the shakings to-and-fro.

The soldiers distributed candies and cold drinks to cheer the civilians.

'Lady, why don't you cut your fingernails?' a stalwart commando asked mock-seriously. 'Your husband will divorce you.'

'Several of the soldiers asked the wakeful people to join in a communal sing-song in an attempt to forget what they had endured, but the civilians were spent and drained of all energy and in no condition for singing.

Rina Cooper went over to one of the young men and asked if any of their number had been killed. He said that he did not know. He was pretending out of a desire not to grieve the questioner. The body of their adored commanding officer, Lieutenant-Colonel Jonathan Netanyahu, was with them on board the aircraft on the way to be interred in the soil of the homeland for which he had laid down his life. The young soldier was lamenting his commander and friend Yoni, who was no more and others of his comrades, too, felt the sadness and despair of that bereavement.

Amos Eran, Director-General of the Prime Minister's Office in Jerusalem, had directed, before the completion of the operation, that a message be transmitted from the Prime Minister, Itzhak Rabin, to the President of the United States:

'Dear Mr President ... We have a common interest in fighting terror. After Israel had arrived at the conclusion that it would not be possible to liberate the passengers of the aircraft who had remained at Entebbe safely from the hands of their captors in any other way, the Government of Israel decided to carry out a military operation, which is going on at this very moment ...'

Ambassador Simha Dinitz in Washington, D.C., through whom the message was sent, received instructions to deliver it only on the day of the action and only after getting the green light from Jerusalem.

The same message contained an assurance from the Prime Minister to the American President that instructions had been given to those responsible for the operation to prevent casualties to the utmost extent possible. Rabin concluded his communication with the request, 'I hope, Mr President, that you will understand the motivations behind this action'.

With the completion of the operation, while the aircraft were still on their way back to Israel, all of the men and officers who had been engaged in 'Operation Jonathan' assembled in the Prime Minister's chambers.

Without further delay the Prime Minister informed the President of the State, Professor Ephraim Katzir, of the liberation of the hostages from the hands of the beasts of prey at Entebbe.

Chief Rabbi Shlomo Goren, Knesset-members Itzhak Navon and Menahem Begin, and all government Ministers received the stirring news from the Prime Minister's lips. The joyous scenes in Rabin's office were mingled with sorrow over the men who had lost their lives.

Towards morning Baruch Bar-Lev picked up the telephone and dialled the number of Idi Amin's home. Ten minutes later he heard the President's voice at the other end of the line.

'Thank you for everything', Bar-Lev said.

'Thanks – for what?' Idi Amin wondered. 'I haven't done anything yet. You must accept the terms of the Palestinians, otherwise you won't get your hostages.'

Burka Bar-Lev smiled to himself. It was apparent that no one had been bold enough to acquaint the President with the latest developments in the situation and the circumstances of the Entebbe operation.

Three hours later the telephone rang. Idi Amin came on the line. With a trembling voice he spoke of 'the friendship that had been betrayed'.

'Your government must be told that it behaved very badly', he urged Bar-Lev.

The short hop from Entebbe to Nairobi was accomplished without incident or difficulty. The 'Hercules' aircraft came down on the airport at M'bakasi near the capital, where it was re-fuelled and prepared for the flight home to Israel.

The trio were joined at Nairobi by a fourth plane, the military 'Boeing 707'. No Ugandan fighter-plane had pursued them and tried to intercept and force-land them.

Three stretchers with wounded were taken off the 'Hercules' and transferred to the field hospital which had been set up on one of the landing circles and manned by twenty-three Israeli doctors. Immediate surgery was performed.

An interesting version was given in this connection by a French reporter at Nairobi, Christian Houche. The report stated among other things:

On Saturday evening, 3 July at 9.30 p.m. (Israel time) a 'Boeing 707' with the Star of David emblem on its tail landed at Nairobi airport and security officers belonging to El Al airlines reinforced by special agents, equipped with 'walkie-talkie' instruments, at once began reconnoitring the vicinity.

Kenyan soldiers guarded the Boeing as they had done twice before that week when an El Al plane had made an intermediate halt at Nairobi. Half an hour later a field hospital was set up at a distance of about thirty yards from the airport. Some thirty people clad in civilian clothes walked around inside.

The Boeing was in wireless contact with the Hercules aircraft. It appeared that these flew along the length of the Red Sea, veered southward and thence turned towards Entebbe without being detected at any time.'

The Government of Israel neither confirmed nor denied the French correspondent's report.

Another item which evoked no official reaction from Israel was carried over the wire service by S.A.P.A., the South African Press Association, stating that a 'Hercules' transport plane with Israeli markings had landed at the end of the week, before the Entebbe action, at Maseru Airport in the territory of Lesotho, and that on 6 July, two days after the action, it was still parked there. Nothing official had been published concerning its arrival.

Eyewitnesses, questioned over the telephone by the Agence France Presse in Johannesburg, confirmed the presence of the aircraft which, according to them, was camouflaged and guarded by local watchmen.

A number of papers outside Israel advanced various surmises concerning the identity of the mysterious plane. Some believed it to be an 'intelligence' plane, others claimed it was a reserve plane for use in an emergency if one of the invading 'Hercules' craft broke down, and one paper even published the theory that it carried commando troops as reinforcements should the coup fail.

The *Los Angeles Times* correspondent in Nairobi cabled his paper that, notwithstanding the denials of Israel and Kenya alike, there was prior agreement between the two countries whereby Israel would be assisted by Kenya in refuelling the planes of the invading force on their way back home, and even make use of Nairobi Airport for the emergency treatment of the many casualties anticipated in the action.

Several of the points adduced by the correspondent in support of his statement were as follows:

• Israeli agents who had been in Nairobi several days made arrangements for the complex operation. An Israeli tourist said, 'There were many Hebrew-speaking young men in my hotel and they were not tourists. The hired cars of his temporary aides were parked closely together outside the Israeli envoy's home'.

- An Israeli 'Boeing 707' fitted out as a field hospital was waiting at Nairobi for the returning people.
- The 'Hercules' planes were re-fuelled before they took the commandos back home, and so was the 'Boeing 707' plane that flew the hostages to Israel.
- Before leaving they were served breakfast in the airport restaurant. A heavy force of Kenyan military police guarded the place. Ambulances waited to take the wounded to hospitals in Nairobi.
- An Israeli guard was placed in the room of one of the Israeli wounded hospitalized in Nairobi. The wounded man was a Haifa resident, aged forty-eight, whose arm was tattooed with a Nazi concentration camp number and who now had a bullet in his shoulder – souvenirs of Nazi and Palestinian persecutions, over an interregnum of thirty years (the reference was of course to Itzhak David. Y.O.).

In the 'Hercules' trio flying out of Nairobi a short while later the liberated passengers sat in the ordinary military seats in company of their liberators, whose faces showed signs of battle fatigue. Nevertheless, the unique *sabra* humour had not deserted them. When the soldiers were asked what was new in Israel and what had happened during the seven 'days of Entebbe', a bearded paratrooper fired back his retort, 'What? Haven't you heard? There's a Value Added Tax now!' Everyone burst into laughter.

One of the civilians expressed loudly his sorrow that the commandos had not been able to lay hands on the great Field Marshal Idi Amin Dada. 'We could have invited him to fly with us to Israel and kept him as out guest for a goodly number of years.'

One of the women passengers approached a soldier sitting erect in a corner and asked, 'Will you allow me to kiss you?' He raised no objection.

At one-third of the flight home the three transport planes

were joined by Israeli fighter-craft which fell into escort formation. Danger still threatened and the escorting fighters were on the alert for any enemy aircraft.

The freed passengers now sat with their heads glued to the small portholes of the 'Hercules' plane. Their eyes roamed over the southern tip of the Sinai Peninsula.

Suddenly they saw far below them Sharm esh-Sheikh, the southern extremity of Israeli territory.

The planes dropped to lower altitude, the runway at the military air base grew larger and in a short space of time they made a smooth landing.

'Flight 139' had come home.

Joseph Haddad, the young man of Bat-Yam, south of Tel Aviv, who had been exercised by thoughts of emigrating from Israel when the French air-bus had taken off from Ben-Gurion Airport a week earlier, gazed with pride at the people who welcomed them at a military air base.

Never would he forget that reception. Everything that had happened to them in Uganda seemed to him like a movie-film. Even the excitement at seeing the Israeli 'Hercules' aircraft landing on the airfield still gripped him.

The thought of emigration from Israel, even for a short while, seemed now to belong to a past era, perhaps to some-one else.

Looking at the crowds and throngs of people delirious with joy, he knew there was no substitute, no substitute whatever for this people of his, brethren with whom 'to dwell together in unity'.

More about Penguins and Pelicans

Penguinews, which appears every month, contains details of all the new books issued by Penguins as they are published. From time to time it is supplemented by *Penguins in Print*, which is our complete list of almost 5,000 titles.

A specimen copy of *Penguinews* will be sent to you free on request. Please write to Dept EP, Penguin Books Ltd, Harmondsworth, Middlesex, for your copy.

In the U.S.A.: For a complete list of books available from Penguins in the United States write to Dept CS, Penguin Books, 625 Madison Avenue, New York, New York 10022.

In Canada: For a complete list of books available from Penguins in Canada write to Penguin Books Canada Ltd, 41 Steelcase Road West, Markham, Ontario.

Whose Jerusalem?

The Conflicts of Israel

Ronald Segal

'This is a book about Israel ... For here is increasingly
evident the contradiction between the idealism of the
pioneers and the prevalent imperatives of the state. Here,
increasingly urgent, is the clash between the covenant with
man and the Covenant with God. Here, the world to
which the society belongs is increasingly challenged by the
world of which the society needs to be a part. Here,
alongside the avowal of a vigorous democracy, is the
politics of an increasingly authoritarian management.
Here, where all Jews were to be brothers together, are
separately the rich and the poor, in an increasing
turbulence of complaint. But here too, in consequence,
may be found the possibilities for a new vitality of vision
that will make of the Return not a mere clinging to the
present ... but the probing of a future to liberate man
from the fear of himself.'

How Israel Lost Its Soul

Maxim Ghilan

The evolution of Israel into an aggressively nationalistic, paramilitary and essentially undemocratic nation has, in Maxim Ghilan's opinion, destroyed any immediate hopes of lasting peace.

Here, in a powerful, thought-provoking book, he charts the events leading up to the birth of the state in 1948, discusses its political and social development and analyses what constitutes 'Jewish identity'. No one can solve the current deadlock overnight (and the latest war illustrates how pertinent it is to the rest of the world). Nevertheless, in his view, unless the international Jewish question can be separated from the Middle East there is little hope for a workable solution.

Writing as a disenchanted 'Middle-Eastern patriot' who believes the Middle East can one day become a 'complex, non-sectarian, multi-cultural, multi-racial United States of the area', Maxim Ghilan allots a heavy responsibility to the part played by Israel in the present conflicts.

The Geography of African Affairs
Fourth Edition

Paul Fordham

The African continent, with its estimated population of 250 million inhabitants living south of the Sahara, measures over 5,000 miles from north to south, and is 2,000 miles wide at the level of the Congo river. Africa thus possesses the rare advantage of sufficient space for economic expansion and development. Technically, however, it lags far behind the rest of the world, owing largely to the physical environment and to the isolation of the individual nations.

In *The Geography of African Affairs* Paul Fordham has tried to 'select from the whole mass of geographical facts about Africa south of the Sahara such information as seems important for the understanding of current political problems'. His book, which includes a number of explanatory maps and tables, provides a clear general survey of Africa, its resources, and problems, followed by detailed studies of each different region. The information it contains is essential to a proper understanding of a continent which has been attracting more and more interest in recent years.

This edition has been fully revised and updated.

The Struggle for the Middle East

The Soviet Union and the Middle East 1958–68

Walter Laqueur

Loans, arms supplies, political assistance, support of the Arab countries against the West and Israel, willingness to cooperate with kings and sheikhs as well as with radical revolutionaries have all helped the Soviet Union to become a Middle Eastern power by invitation. She has seized no bases, but month by month her power and influence grow.

Walter Laqueur is Director of the Institute of Contemporary History and of the Wiener Library, London, and author of our other works on the Middle East, including *The Road to War*, on the Arab–Israeli conflict. In *The Struggle for the Middle East* he reviews Soviet policy in the Middle East during ten important years and analyses its future prospects. He is concerned with the changing moods of Turkey and Iran, the Arab–Israeli conflict, the Russian naval presence, Middle Eastern Communism and the Soviet interest in Persian Gulf oil.

'... the most comprehensive account of Soviet–Middle East relations that has appeared since his own *The Soviet Union and the Middle East* (1959)' – *The Middle East*

Women in the Kibbutz

Lionel Riger and Joseph Shepher

The kibbutzim in Israel offer Israeli women a life that many of their sisters in other societies would consider a hopeless utopian dream: absolute equality, freedom from intense family life, sexual constraints, childbearing if desired, from financial worries and the right – indeed it is demanded of them – to participate in the running of the community.

The authors of this book carefully studied the reactions of three generations of women (in two non-religious collectives) to these radical alternatives in living, with surprising results. The kibbutz has never wavered its goal of equality but, as they show, there is a distinct gap between the real and the ideal. Far from stimulating new social patterns the kibbutz has, in many ways; reinforced the idea of the relative intractibility of the sex roles. This is manifested, for example, in the increasingly 'traditional' polarization of labour and the demand by many women to spend more time with their children.

As the author points out none of these women are downtrodden or mindless; they are, in their opinion, responding to a deeply rooted behavioural pattern – an implication that could have far-reaching effects on the conclusions we draw about society.

Political Murder in Northern Ireland

Martin Dillon and Denis Lehane

Since Stormont was prorogued in 1971 there have been over 200 assassinations in Northern Ireland, many of them involving the torture of their victims. These are killings of people who are not soldiers and cannot be dismissed simply as pathological murders: they are part of a calculated terror campaign and are seen by most sides in the 'Troubles' as legitimate acts of war.

Who is killing whom and why?
How far, for example, is the Army responsible for some of these deaths? Or to what extent do they basically derive from a situation of despairing misery among the Protestant working class, that is equalled only by the misery of the Catholic working class?

This book presents evidence as to how the murders were committed, by whom, and for what purpose: it is based on facts which are available to the press and police but largely ignored. Furthermore it places the killings in the context of the racketeering now endemic in Northern Ireland and shows by what means militants are endeavouring to stop them.

No one who wants to see an end to the horror can afford to ignore a book which topples some of the dearest-held myths of the public in both Britain and Ireland.